# Gunfight At The Old Leake Canal

## GB Hope

Published by GB Hope in the United Kingdom 2016

Copyright GB Hope

http://gbhope9.blogspot.co.uk

ISBN: 978-1533021991

Cover design: Mark Shearman

# 1

*Prince Harry walked slowly along, pushing King Charles in his wheelchair.*

*Little Prince George bravely kept pace, holding his mother's hand; Catherine, Princess of Wales, looking serene in her mourning black. Harry's new wife, Fatima, walked beside her: a comfort.*

*The Prime Minister was present with his cabinet ministers, as were foreign royalty and dignitaries – the US President front and centre, of course. Then came Royal Air Force bigwigs. Celebrities followed behind – Sir David and Lady Beckham front and centre, too, of course. The crowds were ten, twelve deep. Six black horses pulled the gun carriage which bore the coffin, draped in the Royal Standard flag.*

The BBC news coverage cut to a wider angle to include

Westminster Abbey.

In his apartment, in Liverpool city centre, eighteen-year-old Bodie paused the TV, as he went in search of his dropped baseball. Back in his favourite arm chair, the ball again slapping into his baseball glove, he set it on again, fascinated by all things royal. He was wearing only his Adidas trackie bottoms and trainers, as it was a warm Summer's day. He was off college, and not doing a shift as a waiter that day, so had been working out. Bodie did a lot of sport, including Freerunning. As a result, he was in great shape, and his six-pack sat there solidly, even as he slouched.

He scratched his closely cropped head, thinking about taking a shower, but his girlfriend was out of town, on a college archaeology dig, so he was considering just slobbing around – maybe get a curry in. He glanced at a newspaper on the coffee table, with total coverage of the death of Prince William. Assassinated by Islamic State at a polo game in Surrey, the previous week. The country shocked to the absolute core.

It was a free newspaper, as he never had any money to buy one. And he rarely watched the news, what with all the terrorist attacks, almost weekly now, around European cities. And the crazy weather kept flooding Wales and the South West, while there was a drought across America, and the worst ever forest fires in Greece... or wherever; it was hard to keep track. Far too depressing. The world just seemed to be one big miserable, depressing place.

He decided to take a shower, after all. He flipped up from the chair, leaving his glove and ball behind. It was not actually his apartment, but belonged to his older cousin, Anthony, who was a journalist. But the man was rarely there, so it was more of just a place for him and Lily. His girlfriend's framed photo greeted him on entering the bedroom: Lily Fransisca, the same age as him, was an Indonesian student at the nearby university; all jet black hair, black eyes and wide, smiling mouth. The plan was, next time she went back home, he would go with her. He was looking forward to the Asian adventure, and meeting her family, but not the £800 cost of the plane ticket, or the mosquitoes. He blew Lily a kiss, as he found clean boxer shorts.

He heard the door intercom buzzer. He wasn't expecting anybody. He wandered to the front door and looked at the intercom screen, seeing a lone male, who he didn't recognise. He leant on the button. 'Yes?'

'*Hi. Is Anthony there?*'

'No.'

'*Where is he?*'

'He's in Sheffield. Will there be anything else?'

'*Hey, man, let me in.*'

'Why would I want to do that?'

'*I'm a friend of Anthony's.*'

'Are you American?'

'*Yeah. Come on, I need to see him.*' There was a stand-off. '*Anthony Harper. Freelance journalist. Drives a blue Golf. Drinks in the Red Lion pub. He's a friend of mine.*'

Bodie buzzed the man in, opened the front door and went to stand watching the TV. In a moment, Bodie was surprised to be joined by a man in a US Navy uniform. He had no idea on the rank, but the man seemed intelligent. The sailor had a more severe haircut than Bodie, and seemed on edge, looking around.

'Hello, sailor,' said Bodie, with British humour.

'Are you alone?'

'Aye, aye, shipmate.'

'Please just tell me how to find Anthony.'

'Well, you drive to Manchester, head over the Pennine hills, start to feel miserable on entering grim Sheffield, and go to this address I'm going to give you.'

The sailor calmed a little, as Bodie wrote down an address on the pad by the phone.

'Listen, man. My name's Dean. I'm sorry. It's just important.'

'I'm Bodie.'

'Bodie?'

'Tom Bodie. But everyone calls me Bodie.'

'Oh, after the 80's cop show, *The Professionals*?'

*Not heard that one before*, thought Bodie. 'No.'

'So, Bodie, are you related to Anthony?'

'We're cousins.'

'Right. Have you got Anthony's cell number?'

'He's working undercover in a smuggling ring. So, you'll have to go and find him yourself.'

Dean indicated the baseball and mitt on the chair. 'What's your team?'

'No team. I just like playing catch.'

Bodie turned to pass over the slip of paper with the address written on it, but Dean wasn't there any more, instead replaced with a shocking splash of red up the wall. Bodie was momentarily nonplussed, slowly looking down at Dean, with half the man's face missing, then back at the wall which he realised was smeared with the American's blood and brains. Stunned, Bodie allowed his legs to collapse from under him, just as another high calibre bullet came through the window and embedded itself in the wall with a dull thud - Bodie realised that he had actually heard the first bullet, without it registering in his mind. Panic and fear flushed through Bodie's body. He had seen enough Hollywood films to know what was happening. If he could have gained full control of his mind, he would have sworn loudly. Finally, he managed to crawl out of the room. He ended up in his bedroom. *Police!* He had to call the police. He reached up to his bedside table, pulling down his wallet and cell phone. Then he crawled back out of the bedroom. He could hear the hovering helicopter, and it terrified him. His heart was still pumping wildly. He was about to call the police, when he saw four burly men on the door monitor screen, who were not British police officers coming to help. The men were trying to break through the communal door to the apartments. His panic knew no bounds, then, but he forced his mind to work, dragging himself through to the kitchen, at the back of the property, where he could stand and look out - no helicopters, just a view out over the city of Liverpool. He knew he had to get out of the apartment, so climbed through the window and lowered himself down onto the adjoining corrugated roof of a supermarket. He started to run, watching his footing, skipping over air-conditioning units, still hearing the buzz of the hovering helicopter, still fearing instant death.

He reached the edge of the roof. Without hesitation, because he had done it before, he was over the low wall, using his Freerunning skills to bounce from side to side on two walls, a few feet apart, until he reached the ground. Then he had to vault some industrial bins, terrifying a woman member of staff on a cigarette break, before he was walking quickly amongst normal shoppers. He was topless, but that wasn't so strange in Liverpool in the Summertime. He kept moving, looking back occasionally, until he was sure he could not have been tracked.

At last he could stop and think about what had just happened. His heart seemed to empty of blood and he felt his face go cold, even in the hot sunshine - shock, he assumed.

'All right, mate?' asked a girl, in a strong Liverpudlian accent, sitting on a nearby wall with friends.

Bodie tried to use his cell, but it failed.

'Is there no signal?' he asked the girl.

'Nuttink at all. Doing me 'ed in.'

Bodie walked on, and soon began to exit the shopping area, moving on to normal, residential streets. He only happened to be living in Liverpool for his engineering studies; he knew very little about the city. He realised that he knew hardly anybody there, apart from the restaurant where he worked, and his college. The restaurant was closest, so he moved in that direction. He would get help there.

*Murder!* He had been involved in a cold-blooded murder. *Oh my God.*

He came to a stop. Ahead of him there was a garden, with washing hanging out on the line. It all seemed quiet. He decided that he should put a shirt on, as being topless might be spotted from the air better. Without hesitation, he vaulted a wall and, not being a natural thief, made a hurried, random grab at several items. Suddenly, a sunbathing woman screamed at the top of her voice, making Bodie jump out of his skin, before he fled up the street, with the woman's shrieking gradually dying away. Away from the scene of the crime, he discarded two pairs of knickers and a child's football jersey, leaving him with a yellow, flowery shirt to put on.

*Murder!* He thought about it again. But murder from a helicopter. It must be terrorist related, was all he could think. That sailor, Dean, must have... he could hear a helicopter, so he quickly ran to hide under a tree.

Slowly, the sound of the rotors drifted away, so Bodie jogged on. It took him two minutes before he was walking across the car-park of the American diner restaurant and grill where he worked. He went in through the propped-open door, finding the front of house all in gloom, with only one waiter cleaning tables, prior to opening for lunch. The waiter, called Gary, looked up in surprise.

'Ee, ar, Bodie, lad. What brings you in? In your flowery top?'

'Hiya, Gaz. I've come to hand in my notice. Is she in?'

'In the back, there. Watching that funeral.'

Bodie went through to the offices in the back of house. The open door showed his manager, Samantha, sitting watching the State funeral. The middle-aged lady was crying.

'Samantha, hi, I'm sorry to disturb you.'

Samantha indicated the television. 'Isn't it terrible? What a horrible world we live in. And what a horrible shirt. Why are you here, Bodie, you're off today?'

'Is the phone working?'

Samantha checked the phone and nodded. Before Bodie could ask to use it, he heard the sound of squealing car tyres outside. He returned to the restaurant front of house in time to see a man in a black suit talking to Gary.

'Sorry, mate,' said Gary, 'no-one of that name works here, like. I don't think so, anyway. Let me go and ask.'

Gary came towards Bodie, and received just the slightest of head shakes. He turned back to the man. 'Oh, I know who you mean now. He quit the other week. Sorry about that.'

The man pushed past Gary. Either he had seen the little head shake or he was intrigued by the yellow, flowery shirt on Bodie. Bodie stood his ground, waiting to be murdered by gunshot, or, at the very least, detained. The man outweighed him. A crew cut, with the curly communications earpiece just visible. Suddenly, out of nowhere, Bodie's martial arts training came to the fore and he launched a vicious kick to the left side of the man's head, flooring him.

Gary screamed with surprised laughter, 'Woahhh! Where did that come from? Nice one, lad!'

Bodie was straight on top of the man, who was stunned but not completely unconscious. He rifled through his pockets, discarding unimportant items like mints and a nasal inhaler. In a different pocket he found a fold of high value dollar bills, which puzzled him, and then a metal clip with a bullet poking out at the top, which frightened him. He took those two things. Then he found the gun, in its holster under the man's left armpit. He pulled it clear, trying to hide it from Gary, then fled through the back of the restaurant, calling, 'See ya, Gary!'

'Good luck, lad.'

Samantha was nowhere to be seen, so Bodie grabbed her car keys from the desk and burst out through a fire exit, onto the staff car-park.

Bodie drove Samantha's lime-green VW Beetle, with its sunflower on the dashboard, through Liverpool city centre. It was a surreal feeling for Bodie, being amongst people who were having perfectly normal days. He paid to enter a multi-storey car-park and drove up the ramp. Once parked, he looked at the gun and ammunition clip on the passenger seat. Then he put them both in the glove compartment.

Getting out of the car, he savoured a refreshing breeze and looked out over the city. He took out his cell. He had a new message from Lily: *Lincolnshire is like the moon! I miss you. See you soon. Love.*

Wow, what he would give for a cuddle, right then and there. He replied: *I miss you more, baby. Mwah!*

Bodie walked along the lines of parked cars until he came to an almost identical Beetle to Samantha's. After a quick look about him, he ducked down and managed to yank the number plate off. He went to the front of the car and repeated the action, taking both plates back to his car. Next, he took out his cell again and dialled the emergency number: 999.

He waited. 'Police, please.' He waited again. 'Police? My name is Tom Bodie. I want to report a murder. Yes, a murder. Where am I? I'm on the third floor of the car-park on Vernon street.'

With that done, he walked to the edge and dropped his cell to destruction on the pavement below.

# 2

Lily Fransisca was a city girl. Born and bred in Surabaya, Indonesia. Now living and studying in the amazing city of Liverpool, which she had been all around with her new university friends; to the waterfront, the *Beatles* tour, the shopping. Not that she was ignorant of the countryside, having several relatives who lived in more rural areas of Indonesia, and her brother, who had moved to England a few years earlier to be with his English wife, lived in beautiful surroundings, just outside Newbury, in Berkshire. It was just that Lincolnshire was something else; something beautiful and wild and going on forever. Of course, it was a great agricultural area - potatoes, she believed. She had watched the terrain unfold from the University mini-bus, as she and her fellow archaeology club students arrived to start a ten-day dig at a place called Wrangle, near Boston. It was an odd kind of name for a village, but it turned out to be delightful, with friendly people, and their B&B hotel was just the sweetest, 19th century house ever, with ivy across the frontage and original cobbles in the back yard, run by a Mr and Mrs Reeson, both of whom never stopped smiling.

She shared a bedroom with Samia, a chemistry student from Burnley, and they had big black beams running the length of the ceiling and criss-crossing behind their beds, and the floor made Samia feel seasick, it sloped so much. There was Kenny and Ben, along the hall, Rebecca in with teacher, Mrs Dunwoody, and Jack in with Professor Siddiq, the leader of the expedition. They were all having a great time, digging with the Local History Society (under the supervision of experts from Lincoln University) on a newly discovered Roman site. They would have breaks and their lunch in the shade, followed by dinner each evening in the local pub. Not that anyone drank alcohol, especially the Muslims: Lily, Professor Siddiq and Samia. One afternoon, they had even gone to the beach, on The Wash, and there were plans to go to the nearby coastal town of Skegness, if they got the time. So much fun that she occasionally forgot to think about Bodie, back in Liverpool.

She had met Bodie when he and some friends did a Freerunning exhibition on her campus. There had been boyfriends before, but no-one as fit or as interesting as Bodie. She remembered being introduced to him at the end of the show, hot and short of breath (and that had just been her).

*'Bodie? Like in the 80's detective show?'*

*'No.'*

Wow, she wouldn't make that mistake again.

A mutual friend knew where Bodie worked, so they had turned up one night to let him serve them, and found him to be the most incompetent waiter in the history of the world. He had actually dropped a cocktail into a woman's open handbag, and blamed an ear infection for upsetting his balance. Every aspect of their order had been slightly wrong, causing great hilarity. For that he had blamed the morons in the kitchen, but it helped cement their friendship, and he had asked her out as she was leaving. That had been five months ago. She wasn't sure if she loved him, but he was handsome and funny, in a sarcastic kind of way, and he didn't cheat like her previous boyfriend. He was her Bodie. Her wonderful Bodie, and they had been a little intimate, but not actually done it, of course.

Jeez, it was hot at the dig (a different kind of heat to being home in Indonesia). She was in her combat trousers and *Doc Martins* and an old *Vamps* t-shirt that showed a little of her flat mid-riff, which seemed okay while in England. Her wild black hair was contained beneath a black bandana.

They were uncovering a Roman mosaic floor from a bath house. It was a wonderful experience, but hard on the knees and neck. Lily looked along the line; Ben working fastidiously, Kenny drinking from his canteen, Jack showing a bit of builders' bum, Rebecca secretly Whatsapping her boyfriend, who was at Lancaster Uni.

Then she saw Professor Siddiq approaching from the nearby farmhouse. Handsome, gorgeous, heart-flutteringly beautiful, Professor Siddiq. Even in one of those Australian baseball caps with the flap down the back of the neck, and khaki shorts, he was a dream. He was her big, teenage crush, the main reason for her volunteering for that particular expedition.

His face was so smooth, even though he was ancient - surely nearly forty years old. His smile was perfect. He was highly regarded at the university and was very intelligent, but also quite cool. But he was married, to some harlot and awful dentist woman. Lily continued to watch him discreetly through her salty-sweaty eyebrows, pretending to be working.

'What time is it!?' called Professor Siddiq.

'It's lunch time!' they all replied.

Much laughing ensued, as they downed tools and headed towards their backpacks in the shade. Lily quenched her thirst from her canteen and bumped hips with Rebecca, 'Is he still missing you?'

'Sort of. He's playing cricket.'

'Oh, well, no girls at the cricket.'

'There had better not be.'

Professor Siddiq had made a bee-line for Lily. She was startled, blushing, although he didn't seem to notice. Rebecca smirked and moved away.

'Lily, I just wanted to tell you, you are doing very well, for only your second dig.'

'Thank you, Professor Siddiq.'

'Lily, I told you, out in the field, it's okay to call me Salman.'

'I... err... just feel that might be a bit... you know... inappropriate.'

He smiled. 'As you wish. Lily, there was something I wanted to ask of you.'

He seemed a little awkward, all of a sudden. Lily waited, telling herself to breathe. She crossed her arms over her chest then quickly took them down again.

'Yes, Professor?'

'Well, as you know, the children from the local school are

coming to visit the dig this afternoon. I wondered if you would be so good as to handle them with me? You are naturally charming and patient, unlike me. I would be very grateful.'

Lily beamed from ear to ear. 'I'd love to do that!'

'That's great. Thank you. Right, off you go to your lunch.'

'Okay. Thank you.'

Lily watched him move off towards fellow teacher, Mrs Dunwoody, who was also dressed for the Aussie Outback. Delighted, Lily joined the others in the shade. Rebecca and Samia teased her a little bit, while the boys were none the wiser.

Bodie had driven the Beetle out of the car-park. He parked it across the road from the entrance to the multi-storey and got out to lean on the bonnet to wait. At one point he had to look away quickly, as an image of the blood-stained wall flashed into his head. He determined to pull himself together.

He didn't have to wait long. But, instead of one or two marked police cars rushing to detain someone who had reported a murder, he was treated to the worrying spectacle of three black Range Rovers, with blacked-out windows, arriving at speed and whizzing up the ramp into the car-park. Very sinister, indeed.

He got into the Beetle and drove off. Soon, he noticed that his bimbo manager had left the car with almost no fuel, so he pulled into the first petrol station that he saw. He filled up, before going in to pay with his *Visa* card. He also bought a packet of cheese and onion crisps, which he proceeded to eat, while he used the outside cash machine. Moving towards the

Beetle, he suddenly heard the sound of the helicopter again, seemingly immediately overhead. Quickly, he grabbed the gun and ammunition from the glove compartment and bolted away. If he had driven out, he just knew they would have been straight onto him. Instead, he ran through the garage car wash, skipped a low wall, and was away across wasteland.

Ahead was a graveyard, with leaning birch trees, and then a pale, sunlit church. Ringing bells competed with the whirr of the rotor blades - although, in his fear, the sound of the helicopter might have been in his head. Bodie leapt a stone wall, vaulted a low crypt, hurried between the grave stones. All he could hear was bells, so he slowed to a jog, believing that the helicopter had failed to follow him again.

Unfortunately, he found himself jogging through a wedding party as the people exited the church, *sorry, sorry,* and then he was out onto an unknown road. He was panting hard. If he hadn't been so fit, then the sheer stress of the morning would have defeated him. But what to do now? What on earth to do? What he needed was his cousin, Anthony.

# 3

Anthony Harper, freelance journalist, was in the Manor area of Sheffield, South Yorkshire. Actually, by bizarre coincidence, he had been born there, twenty-five years earlier, but he no longer knew a single soul in the area. He was an only child, his parents had been retired in New Zealand since 2010, and he had left all his friends behind when they departed Sheffield at fourteen. Perhaps there were some old school friends who might recognise the name, but certainly not the powerfully built man he had grown into, and he currently wore a heavy beard.

He was unknown to the public, but in the newspaper business he was thought of as an up-and-coming name, who had done good pieces on varied subjects as: inner-city gangs, badger-baiting and the fracking industry. One or two times he had been beaten up, and he was like the Patrick Swayze character in the film, *Road House*, in so much as he never took his own car on a job, as it was certain to get its tyres slashed.

It was cloudy and humid in Sheffield. He was in one of those tee-shirts favoured by bodybuilders to emphasise their physique, as he was going for the intimidating look. His head was shaved, which had been the biggest wrench in getting into character; and that character was Handler - he handled the first step of illegal immigrants arriving in the South Yorkshire area. Or, at least, he pretended to for the last month, after making connections with the main Handler, a man called Findlay, who for his own reasons wanted the gang exposed (but drew the line at approaching the police). A deal had been made, Anthony had been schooled in the role and then thrown himself into the job. He was just in the stage of gathering information and building trust. He was soon planning to go with the secret camera, where it got really risky.

So, there he was, going by the name of Tony, waiting for a group of illegals to exit a lorry and be put into a set of rooms within a disused warehouse. The first few times he had done that, so far, he had met members of the crew, who were a mixture of English and Romanians. This was the first time he had encountered the Mr Big. He was an Englishman, in his fifties, with a non-descript accent, going by the name of Henry. Anthony had shaken the offered hand, expressed surprise that the man would ever want to be at the sharp end of the operation. Henry had laughed, leant into his black Porsche Cayenne, and retrieved a camera and a bottle of water. Anthony held his tongue. But he watched Henry closely.

The lorry driver threw up the back shutter with a great clatter, and Anthony spotted several huddled figures behind pallets of electrical equipment.

Henry took Anthony's photo, much to his surprise. 'Hey!' he complained. 'What's the game?' He tried to walk a fine line between being upset and showing respect.

Henry laughed. 'You're such a handsome man, Mr Tony. Handsome, indeed.' Then he stopped the big group of scruffy illegals from disembarking all at once, and took on a fussy, "controlling the scene" kind of demeanour, like a film director. 'You, my man,' he said to a puzzled teenager of Middle Eastern origin, handing him the bottled water. 'You, get down, start drinking.' The youth didn't understand, so Henry mimed the drinking action and the youth obliged. 'Stand there. You, young man, out! Stand there. Woman with baby, start to hand baby down to this young man.'

Anthony watched on with morbid fascination at the unfolding pantomime.

'Wait!' called Henry. 'Stop with baby. Everyone look this way. You!' He turned to the first youth. 'Dribble. A long dribble of spit.' The youth had no idea what was going on. Henry took back the water bottle, filled his mouth and started to dribble it on the floor, standing deliberately like a wide-boy, like a cheeky young thug. The youth realised what was expected of him. Henry jumped back with camera in hand. 'Do you see, Mr Tony? A marvellously miserable scene. Almost apocalyptic. You, boy, dribble! You, baby handed down! Eyes, everyone, on me!' And he started clicking away at the grim scene. 'Fantastic! Jolly good.' Then he was making to leave, stopping, turning back. 'Tony, I'm loving your work, by the way. They are all yours. I'm off to the golf course now.' And with that, Henry climbed into his Porsche and sped away.

Later that day, Anthony made sure he wasn't being followed by anyone, in his leased BMW 3 series, and drove south to the Woodseats area of the city. He parked at a row of shops, and went into a newsagents for some mints and a Lottery ticket. Next door was a *Subway* shop, so he chose to go in for a late lunch. He had showered and changed into a less intimidating shirt. His beard still itched and he couldn't wait to shave it off. He checked the cell phone that he was currently using, but found no messages.

After his meal, he drove around into a run-down housing estate and parked up. There were a lot of feckless teenagers wandering around the estate. The woman he was seeing happened to be outside her home, with her toddler son in her arms, talking with a man, who he assumed was the child's father. She saw him, and her face lit up. Anne-Marie, single-mother, unemployed, living in a council flat, but the prettiest little creature he had ever known. She was blonde, with a delicate jaw; teasingly, her pink top was pulled down to reveal her left shoulder. He approached slowly. He had not meant to start anything romantic while undercover in Sheffield; it had just happened, in a City Centre bar. Even more than removing his beard, he longed to be able to tell her who he really was, and perhaps get her to move in with him.

The man departed. He did look at Anthony, but without any sign of aggression.

'Hi, Tony,' said Anne-Marie, smiling.

'Hello, you.' He indicated the man. 'Your little one's father?'

'Yeah, it is. There's no problem, though. Won't you come in?'

'Thank you.'

Anthony said hello to the small child, and followed Anne-Marie inside. She had the small house decorated in a nice way, with an *IKEA* feel to all the furniture. The child was put down into his playpen and Anne-Marie asked if he wanted a cup of tea. They stepped through to the kitchen, where he pressed her up against a counter. She liked that a great deal.

'I've missed you, baby,' she said.

'I've missed you more.'

'Can you stay for a while?'

'Sure.'

She smiled and caressed his beard, and then they tenderly kissed.

Over in Wrangle, the university archaeology team were taking a well-deserved break. Lily had all three of the boys sunbathing (fully clothed) beside her, and Rebecca was engrossed in texting her boyfriend, so she turned her attention to Professor Siddiq and Samia, who were discussing her family's grocery business, at home in Burnley. The Professor was without his hat, but wore sunglasses up on the top of his head. Lily could see a tuft of hair sticking up from inside his shirt collar, and there was a scar on his left forearm - how she would like to run her finger along that. She sipped her water, looked at the clouds. How could she make Samia go away? She wanted him to only talk to *her*.

'Oh, God, Lily,' said Professor Siddiq. 'It's that time already.'

Pleeeease help.'

Lily jumped out of her romantic reverie. 'Eh? I'm sorry?'

He was pointing towards the approaching class of Primary school children, shepherded by two teachers, arriving to visit the dig. Lily laughed. They both stood up, brushing grass from their trousers.

'Oh, Professor, how did you get to be where you are in education, I wonder? I'll deal with them. Oh, look, they're so small and cute. Can I keep one?'

'I shall have a word with the teaching staff for you.'

'But I'm too young to adopt. You don't have any children, do you, Professor? Don't you want one?'

'Well, if I was to have one of those I would have to do some serious vetting.'

Lily looked at him, puzzled. 'Why?'

'Because, my dear Lily, I'm only prepared to take on a child who can quickly earn ten million pounds at either tennis or golf.'

They both laughed happily together.

# 4

Police Constable, Karl Cromwell, flipped a *tic-tac* mint into his mouth, before heaving his 240 lbs bulk from his patrol car. He knew he was overweight, and without a prayer when it came to chasing down a suspect, but as long as his bosses employed 98 lbs, five-foot-five females, who were ignored by criminals and all manner of low-life, and got flattened at the first bit of argy-bargy outside the local pubs, then he needn't worry too much.

He was the Community Bobby, and in Purley-on-Thames, Berkshire, to investigate reports of an abandoned stolen trials bike on the river bank. But there was no rush. Time to put his hat on and wander over to chat with old Mr Hearns about the astro turf he had put down in his small front garden.

'Saves on mowing, I suppose, Mr Hearns.'

'It does, Karl. It does, indeed. But, tell me, does it look silly?'

'Not at all. Not at all. I'm considering it myself, I'm so fed up with paperboys and menu-posting idiots traipsing all over my front lawn. Are you well?'

'I can't complain.'

Mrs Jameson, from across the road, came out to speak to him.

'And how are you, Mrs Jameson?'

'I'm very well, PC Cromwell. But I have a complaint.'

'Do you, really?'

'Yes, this road, PC Cromwell. This little, suburban road you see before you. Now, do you think it needs an ice cream van... every... single... night? With its stupid chimes blaring out?'

'I'm not sure I have an answer for you on that one, Mrs Jameson. But I'll look into it.'

'If you would be so kind.'

'Well, if you'll excuse me, I must try to find this stolen bike, down by the river.'

He waddled off in the direction of the Thames. It was a hot day and he felt the first prickling of sweat under his white shirt. He could do with an ice cream, actually, right then and there. He left the tarmac of the road, down through some shrubbery, glad of the shade. The Thames faced him, moving calmly along. It was a pleasant sight. He took off his hat, adjusted his utility belt, and moved along the pathway. Across the river, he exchanged a wave with a woman walking her two dogs.

He soon found the trials bike, abandoned in weeds, and examined it for damage caused by the joyriders. To his limited knowledge, it looked okay. Then he was worried about having to push it up to the road - that would have him sweating buckets. While he was contemplating that unpleasant task, a canal boat began to drift by. PC Cromwell straightened up and turned, expecting to say hello to the people on board. But the boat looked to be unmanned, which was very puzzling.

'Hello, there! You, on the boat!'

Slowly, the boat angled towards the far bank and came to a crashing halt. PC Cromwell waited to see if anyone emerged from below decks, but nobody did. He was disturbed by then, just reaching for the walkie-talkie, near his left shoulder. But before he could call base, one of those eight-man rowing skulls came drifting along, with eight lifeless rowers slumped over the oars.

'Oh, Christ!'

PC Cromwell discarded his utility belt and stab vest before plunging into the river. Huffing and puffing, he pulled the boat in by the bow and secured it to the bank. Then he went from one young rower to the next checking for vital signs, and found none. He reached for his radio and screamed for assistance. Then he started dragging the men out of the boat. Exhausted, he stopped after the third man was lying lifeless on the ground and started moving between them, doing First Aid. 'Help!' he screamed towards the houses. 'Someone help me!'

The weather in Liverpool was absolutely wonderful: wall to wall sunshine, and a refreshing breeze. Feeling the unwanted start of a suntan, Bodie walked onto a supermarket car-park, moving towards the entrance doors, while trying to look as nonchalant as possible. He watched shoppers coming and going with their trolleys. He saw one lady loading the boot of her Audi A3, and veered off towards her. The instant that he saw the keys in the ignition, he was in to the driver's seat and driving the car away, leaving the woman screaming and running futilely after him. Bodie drove out of the car-park, but the tail-gate was still up and it smashed into the height restriction barrier with a massive crash and a shattering of glass.

'Dammit!'

He drove away at speed and turned into smaller side streets. Then he pulled up, so he could get out and shut the boot. That's when he heard a noise, and slowly looked to the rear seats. There, showered in glass, but uninjured, sat a baby in a car-seat.

'Dammit.'

Bodie carefully lifted the baby out of the car. By then, he was attracting some attention from the locals and passers by. It would not be long before someone challenged him. Looking about, he selected a nice-looking older lady and presented her with the child.

'I've just stolen this car. There was a baby inside. You must call the police.'

The woman became flustered but her natural impulse kicked in, and she took the child and moved away from the crazy man. Bodie shut the tailgate, jumped in and drove away from there quickly.

A few minutes later, he drove onto a different supermarket car park and went slowly up and down the rows of parked vehicles, looking for a similar Audi, so he could do his changing number plates trick again. He did consider trying to steal another car, so that he didn't have one with a broken back window, but the stress of having to try that again put him off doing it. He spotted a suitable target and parked nearby. But, when he approached the other Audi, he realised that the cars were newer than the Beetle, and he would need a screwdriver. He returned to his stolen car and rooted about in the boot. Some of the woman's shopping appealed to him, so he nibbled *Hobnob* biscuits and drank orange juice, until he found a screwdriver in the spare wheel cavity. He quickly went about his task, and was ready to depart, closing the tailgate.

'What's going on here, then?'

Bodie spun around, expecting to see the police, or store security. Instead, he found a little, old man just being nosy over the shattered window. It was a relief.

'Vandals,' answered Bodie, matter-of-factly.

'It's shocking, isn't it. I tell you, the country's going to the dogs.'

'I know. I know. Terrible, isn't it? Well, if you'll excuse me, I'm off to get it fixed now.'

'Okay. Good day to you, young man.'

'Good day.'

Bodie drove away and headed out of the city. Within a few minutes, he was on the M62 motorway driving towards Manchester, and from there he would go on to Sheffield.

It was a bit draughty, having no back window. He stayed in the inside lane, trying not to attract attention to himself. Luckily, the motorway was fairly quiet. It took about thirty minutes, and then he came towards the M60, choosing to head east and then enter the city from the south. Traffic began to build up. He passed under a motorway sign which directed him towards Manchester Airport, Birmingham and The South. He looked back and was pleased to see that he was being followed by an elderly lady driver in a Nissan Micra, not someone who was likely to call the police on him, even if she had noticed the damage.

As he started to go up onto the Barton Bridge there was a contraflow system in place, with millions of red and white traffic cones. There were massive cranes visible at the side of the bridge - *they were always doing something*! The traffic began to slow. At the top, he had to come to a stop, causing him to curse. Then he waited. But nobody moved. He saw that there was a family in a People Carrier in the lane beside him, several articulated lorries ahead and behind. Finally, after about ten minutes, people started to get out of their vehicles to try to look ahead over the crest of the bridge. It was assumed there had been an accident.

Bodie got out of his car to look at the line of stopped vehicles. Over to his left he could see the Manchester Ship canal, winding its way into the distance, and, ahead, stood the domes of the Trafford Centre shopping mall. A plane passed over, but it was only a private Cessna, coming in to land at the nearby Barton Aerodrome.

One driver called to another, 'There'll be an impromptu football game on here soon. There always is.' They both laughed.

Bodie moved over to the hard shoulder, seeing how scarily far down the dirty canal was.

'Don't do it!' shouted a woman driver.

'I'm sorry?' asked Bodie, turning.

She was smiling. 'Don't jump. It's not that bad yet.'

Bodie smiled at her joke. 'I suppose it's just the bridge repairs holding us up? Or an accident?'

'No, no. My husband is a few minutes ahead, in his own car. He just sent me a text, saying there's one of those police terrorist checkpoints at the end of the bridge. The police are checking every car.'

He kept his face straight. 'Oh, right.'

Bodie wandered around, thinking hard. If it was a terrorist check, then maybe he would be waved through. But he knew, more likely than not, he would be detained as soon as they saw the shattered window, and then they would find the gun in the car. More people were milling about. Frustrated HGV drivers slouched on their driving wheels.

Then Bodie saw armed police in the distance, working their way up through the cars. His mind began to whirl. He collected the gun and ammunition clip, put them in his pocket, and moved away from the Audi, walking actually in the direction of the police. Before they could notice him, he went over the side of the bridge. Several drivers did see him go, however, and began shouting to him. Bodie landed on a service walkway. One of the cranes was very close, all red metal, very imposing. There was perhaps a four foot gap between where he was standing and a base which held the control cab. Without hesitation, Bodie leapt the space, then swung under a rail. *Wow*, he thought, ultimate Freerunning. He quickly found the trap door which led to the ladder, but it was locked from beneath. Panic gripped him momentarily, fear of being detained, before he checked all about him. He would have to go out onto the crane, then down and back across to rejoin the ladder underneath the cab. Bodie looked out along the crane to the shopping centre, bright in the sun, and to the hills in the distance, then down through the crossed metal bars to the canal and fields below. It was terrifying. He had climbed things before, buildings and walls, but never anything like that. He gulped away a brief feeling of nausea. Then, he started to climb down through, hanging momentarily, trying to feel for the thin walkway between the struts. The metal was slightly damp from earlier rain - *madness, Bodie, madness.* His left hand came off and he was hanging from certain death by just the right. Using all his fitness, and having the fearlessness of youth, he forced himself up to get both hands gripping again.

He knew he could drop, but the fear factor kept him holding on, making him look down, sensing the void below. He felt like one of those total nutcases who hang off cranes and tall buildings just for fun. Then he let go and his feet felt the security of the metal below. He could hear the wind all about him but he was somewhat protected by the side of the bridge. Perhaps the police above had been alerted, by then, but he didn't know, he just moved cautiously along the lower half of the crane, went through a hatch, and started to descend the ladder.

At the bottom, he saw contractors' huts and construction vehicles, a few workers in their hi-viz jackets, but nobody seemed to notice him. He looked up, and that was when the adrenalin really hit him - it was so, so high - a monstrosity of a construction, blocking out the sun. Weak in the knees, Bodie walked away from the site.

# 5

It was a glorious day in the city of Le Claire, Iowa.

Postman, Pete Mosby, was happily working on his tan, as he walked his usual route, which, at one point, took him down to the banks of the Mississippi river. He was a forty-six-year-old, father of four, who was thinking about all the normal stuff in life, such as what to get his wife for their 21st anniversary? What he thought about his oldest girl's latest deadbeat boyfriend? Whether he should ever buy another Volkswagen?

Folks were normally very civil towards him, and he enjoyed his job - only once threatened with a firearm, and only one dog-bite scar collected in twenty-three years' service. He stopped to chat with a couple of storekeepers, who were shooting the breeze, and exchanged pleasantries with Mr and Mrs Jacobson, as they left for work. He then rang the doorbell for a Miss Gordon, as he had a package for her. The lovely young lady skipped to the door in just her pyjamas and made his day with her gorgeous smile.

'Now, Miss Gordon, have you won more stuff in those competitions you enter?'

'It looks like it. I'm extraordinarily lucky. Thank you, Pete. You have a nice day.'

'You too, Miss Gordon.'

He moved on, taking a bend in the road. Although he was daydreaming again, he was a little puzzled to see dark objects on the ground, far ahead, but he carried on and delivered more mail. Walking nearer to the mysterious shapes, he tried to make out what they were. Suddenly, he stopped, realising that it was people lying in the street. He ran forward. Four, five, seven, nine bodies in total. The scene was horrific. He dropped his mail sack and ran for help.

Bodie had only ever been to Manchester once before, and, as he remembered, he didn't like it very much. He rode a bus from the Stretford area and got off when the driver told him he was near to his destination, which was Deansgate, one of the main thoroughfares through the city centre. It turned out to be a ludicrously long walk before he finally saw the bicycle courier office that he was looking for. The office had a very small sign on the door - so tiny that he had been lucky not to miss it. There was a passageway through to the rear of the premises, which was practical for the bikes. He stepped inside the building, feeling his feet stick to the carpet, and waited for an unshaven, bored-looking man to get off the phone and raise his doleful eyes at him.

'I'm sorry to bother you,' said Bodie. 'I'm looking for a Dan

Tisdall. Does he still work here, and is he on today?'

The man took a lazy look at the clock on the wall. 'Ah, Dan the man. Well, he's been ninety minutes going to Ardwick and back, probably stopped off for a bite of lunch on the way, so he should be back soon. Unless, you see, he's decided to do a spot of shopping in Debenhams, by any chance.'

Bodie found the man's sarcastic attitude highly amusing, although he kept his face straight. 'Thank you.' He stepped back away from the counter, looking at the TV news on the nearby television. 'Has anything new happened?'

'Only in Moscow.'

'Moscow? So, nothing in Liverpool? No shootings from helicopters? Nothing like that?'

The man raised a puzzled eyebrow. 'No. Have you been having bad dreams?'

'Yeah, something like that.'

Bodie went back out onto the Deansgate pavement to wait. He watched the traffic and the city centre workers go by. A few couriers came and went, via the passageway. Then a BMX arrived at speed. The rider had a hippy thing going on, with a goatee beard and wild hair poking through his crash helmet. His top was psychedelic and his courier satchel appeared to have been knitted from yak wool. The man smiled as he recognised his friend. Bodie grinned at Dan, his boyhood best pal from Sheffield.

'Hey, Bodie! What brings you here, man!?'

They embraced.

'Dan, mate, you won't believe what brings me here. You're looking good, anyway. Can we go somewhere to talk? Unless you're busy right now.'

'No, no, all the time in the world. Are you in a car? No? Well, I'll get you some wheels and we'll go for a coffee.'

Dan Tisdall was eighteen, like Bodie. His family had relocated to Manchester a couple of years earlier. He was not particularly academically minded, but he loved skateboarding and riding his BMX, so it was inevitable that he would drift into a bicycle courier job, or the like. He and Bodie had got into Freerunning together while at school. They were quite close, despite life getting in the way of their friendship.

Dan borrowed another BMX from the sardonic man behind the desk, who Dan introduced as Kevin. 'I believe you've met my old mate. This is Bodie.'

'Bodie? From that 80's TV show?'

Dan and Bodie rode off into the back streets of Manchester. They jumped kerbs, cut across pedestrianised areas, generally behaved in a very laddish manner, until Dan skidded to a stop outside a little café, where other bikes were propped up against the wall.

The salt and pepper condiments were rattling against the ketchup bottle, as Dan hit his forehead repeatedly on the table. All the other customers in there knew Dan, so paid him little or no attention. Dan sat up and stared again at Bodie, aghast at what his friend had just whispered to him.

'Jeez, man,' said Dan, 'you're not kidding, are you?' He got up, walked about, paused to look quizzically at the novel that one of his fellow couriers was reading on his break, then sat back down, resting his face on his hands. 'That's heavy, Bodie.'

That's a freakin' film. What, so...' he lowered his voice, '...they killed this American guy because he was trying to talk to Anthony?'

'And when I called the police, they sent this Special Forces crew, in black Range Rovers.'

'I'm amazed, pal. I am totally stunned. So, tell me, what do you need from me?'

'I need a legal vehicle. I need to get to Sheffield, to speak to Anthony. He'll know what to do. We'll go to his editor, or a Member of Parliament, or something.'

'All right. We'll take my mum's car. I'm insured for it. It's nothing much, though.'

'We?'

Dan grinned. 'Of course, mate. I'm coming along.'

Early evening, at Cawang railway station, in South Jakarta, Indonesia, eighteen-year-old Yenny Nardi was on her way home after college. It had been a ridiculously stressful day. She thought she was coming down with a cold, too, and her mother had been too busy at work to give her a ride home - selfish woman, who would still expect a birthday present at the weekend, no doubt. But, anyway, Yenny was content, happily engrossed in texting her secret Australian "boyfriend", giggling away to herself. She moved through the station on auto-pilot. It was just a five minute walk home from there, and then she could eat some noodles and have a much needed long shower. A textbook slipped from under her arm. She stopped and bent to pick it up, then hoisted her shoulder bag and stepped outside into the still humid early evening. She laughed, as 19-

year-old Stuart, in Perth, was being particularly naughty. She was typing a response when she realised that something was different, out there. After a moment, she realised that there was no traffic noise. Nothing at all. She raised her eyes up from her iPhone, and struggled to believe the scene that faced her - normally, outside the station, it would have been buzzing with motorbikes and cars. But all she could see were half a dozen motorbikes or scooters lying on their sides, alongside their riders. The riders were not moving at all, and neither were several prone pedestrians. Yenny was instantly terrified and confused. She retraced her steps and went in search of someone. Anyone.

Dan led Bodie up the concrete stairs and into his bedsit apartment, in the Hulme area of Manchester.

'Home sweet home,' said Dan. 'So, Bodie, tell me what do you think?'

Bodie appraised the place in less than two seconds. 'What a cesspit.'

'I know, I know, but it's cheap and gets me away from the folks. Make yourself comfortable. It was a good idea to rent this place when I had a girlfriend.'

'You brought a girl *here*? How low were her standards?'

'Pretty non-existent, to date me. You want coffee?'

Bodie nodded and sat down. In doing so, he took the gun out of the back of his belt and put it on a table.

Dan laughed. 'You carry it at your back? Classic style.' He picked up the gun. 'It's a serious piece of hardware. It's a Sig Sauer. There's the safety catch. See?'

'You're a gun expert now?'

'More than you, Sunshine. We should try it, on the way to Sheffield.'

'Try it? As in practice? Like it's to be used for real? I suppose you're right. It might come to that.'

Dan put the gun down with a thud and went over to make coffee.

'After you've had this,' said Dan, 'the shower's through there, and I'll get you some clean clothes.'

'Okay, mate. Hey, Dan. Thank you for this.'

'No worries.'

They spent the evening by going out to a nearby Curry house. Dan had the chicken vindaloo, while Bodie played safe with the chicken biryani, washed down with a few beers. Then, once back in the bedsit, they watched TV for a few hours, deliberately not talking about the situation they were embroiled in, and then when Bodie fell asleep in the chair, Dan went to bed.

They woke early for some breakfast of coffee and bowls of dry Corn Flakes, as all the milk had gone into the coffee. Bodie was in a pair of Dan's jeans and a heavy charcoal-grey top. He felt clean and refreshed, and ready to push on to Sheffield. They stepped out of the apartment building into light rain (Manchester being famous for rain), and went over to a nearby bus stop, joining several miserable commuters.

'Let's go and get mother's car, then,' said Dan.

'Are you sure she won't mind?'

'Yeah, I'm sure. She only uses it to go to the shops, once a week. Hey, I had ancestors living right round here, you know, back in the early 1900's.'

'Did you?'

'Yeah, I looked them up on one of those ancestry sites. Obviously, it was completely different here back then, before the Germans bombed it and then the rest was torn down in the Sixties. Yes, the famous Tisdall night soil men.'

'The what?'

'Sewage.'

A bus stopped and the commuters started to get on.

'Oh, I didn't ask,' said Dan, 'Are you still with that Lily girl?'

'Yeah. Lily's good. So, what happened with your girlfriend?'

'She just decided to dump me. On Christmas Day.'

'On Christmas Day? Ouch.'

They both had a good laugh.

The bus took them to Chorlton-cum-Hardy, where they got off and walked to Dan's family home, a 1930's semi-detached. Only his mother was in. She recognised Bodie immediately, gave him a kiss, and took them both through to the kitchen, where she was in the middle of baking, on every available surface.

'God, Mum, are you practising for *The Great British Bake Off*?'

'No, just making things for your Aunt Karen's school fete.'

Dan made tea, while he asked to borrow the car, saying they were going to see friends in Sheffield.

'Bodie, have you eaten?' asked Mrs Tisdall.

'Yes, thank you, Mrs Tisdall. We've had breakfast.'

'I'm sure it wasn't very sufficient. I do worry about him, you know, at that terrible place. You know, they had a drugs raid in the flat above, recently. You'll stay for lunch, of course, before you set off?'

'Yes, thank you.'

'You will look after him in Sheffield?'

'I promise, Mrs Tisdall.'

Dan showed Bodie the car, which was a metallic purple Ford Fiesta with a charity *Red Nose* on the front grill. Then they kicked a football around the back garden for a while, before Mrs Tisdall had done them some soup and sandwiches.

By noon, they were on their way, heading through the town of Stockport and up into the hills. They got onto the Snake Pass, and the little Fiesta bobbed along quite well. It was barren up there: a road which was often closed during bad Winter weather. After about half an hour, Dan pulled into an empty lay-by and switched off the engine. They got out of the vehicle.

'Time to practise,' said Dan.

They waited for a petrol tanker to trundle by, then jumped a little fence and moved down into a small copse.

'One shot each,' said Dan. 'No need to waste ammo.'

'Ammo, what a word. This is insane.'

Dan fiddled with the Sig Sauer, then he aimed the weapon, steadied himself and fired into a tree. A broad grin spread across his face and he wished he could continue. But he passed the gun over to Bodie, who blinked with nerves as he took it. Bodie weighed the gun in his hand, brought it up, prepared himself and fired off his one shot. He missed his intended target, but had at least used the weapon. Dan took it back and made it safe. It had taken less than a minute but for two normal English guys it had been a big deal, indeed.

# 6

Lily creaked across the ancient floorboards of the B&B hotel and came down into the breakfast room, smiling at everyone; everyone except Professor Siddiq, who was disappointingly absent - causing her mood to sink. She had done her hair in a different way, pulled to the left, with hair clips, especially for him. She said hello to a smiling Mrs Reeson, the owner, who was coming in with fresh toast, and sat down next to Samia, pouring herself a cup of coffee.

Samia dug her in the ribs, indicating for her to look through the open French windows, where two donkeys were nosing over the fence from an adjacent farmer's field. An American couple, who were also staying at the B&B, were petting the animals. Lily smiled, and asked if everyone had slept well.

A message came through on Rebecca's cell, making Lily think of Bodie. She had told him she would probably be fairly incommunicado while in Lincolnshire, but he was still being frugal with his messages. Maybe he was out with the boys from college. She stopped fretting, as Professor Siddiq entered the room. He sat right down beside her.

'Good morning, Lily,' he said.

Lily felt a thrill run up her spine, but she also sensed a sombre tone in his voice and, under the cover of the boys getting up, had a good look at his face.

'Is everything all right, Professor?'

He reached for the marmalade to put on his toast. 'Oh, just the news. Yet another terrorist attack.'

'Oh, where is it this time?'

'In Rotterdam.'

'I'm sure they'll beat them eventually, Professor.'

Professor Siddiq smiled at her. 'I'm sure you're right, Lily. Maybe I shouldn't watch the news while we are at this beautiful place.'

'It is beautiful, and no, you shouldn't.'

'Oh, hey, look at the donkeys.'

Lily looked again and saw that the American tourists had gone. 'Let's go and see them.'

'Yes, we must.'

Mrs Dunwoody was leaving with Samia and Rebecca. 'Catch us up, Salman.'

'Yes, Elaine, right along in a moment.'

Lily and the Professor went out into the morning glare. Lily easily imagined that it was her own English country garden and she was taking a morning stroll with her new husband, Salman.

'I think you've had a lot of fun, Lily.'

'I have, Professor. It's been amazing.'

They reached the docile donkeys and began stroking their faces.

'I don't really want to go back to Liverpool now,' said Professor Siddiq. 'If I'm being completely honest.'

'But your wife will be missing you.'

'My wife? Yes, I suppose she will. But, between you and me, Lily, she's quite a cold woman.'

'I'm sorry to hear that. Was it an arranged marriage?'

'No, no, the error was all mine.' He chuckled. 'Anyway, do you miss home, at all?'

'I try not to fret about it. I miss my mum, of course. And I miss the food - well, to be honest, I miss eating with my fingers. I miss the rice. The milk and butter and stuff is all better here, but not the rice. And as for the noodles. We have the best noodles in the whole world.'

Professor Siddiq laughed. 'You're making me hungry again. Let's get on, we have a long day ahead of us. Hopefully, the rain will stay off.'

Lily stumbled on a tuft of lawn, and felt the Professor's steadying hand on her lower back. *Electrifying.* Then they headed back inside to gather their hats and canteens.

Everything was packed and everyone sitting in the mini-bus by the time they came outside. Lily felt a little embarrassed, but excited still, and she even got a helping hand from Professor Siddiq up into the vehicle.

Professor Siddiq got behind the wheel, with Mrs Dunwoody alongside him, and he pulled away from the B&B. Rebecca played music on her cell, and they were all in good spirits.

When they arrived at the dig, all the local volunteers were drinking tea and chatting about a discovery of a statue, the previous evening. Lily and Samia went straight to their section of trench, unpacked their tools and sat themselves down with their feet dangling over the edge.

'Well?' asked Samia.

'Well what?'

'You went outside with him.'

'Just to stroke the donkey.'

'Is that a euphemism?'

Both girls screamed with laughter and fell back onto the grass.

Finally, they regained their composure and set to work. After a few minutes, Lily felt a shadow move across her. She looked up to see a man and a woman standing there, admiring the mosaic floor.

'Hi,' said Lily, shielding her eyes.

The woman spoke, with an American accent. 'Oh, hi. Sorry to disturb you. We were just fascinated by this archaeology thing.'

'Yes, isn't it marvellous?'

'Sure is,' answered the man. 'I'm sorry, I'm Harrison. This is my wife, Irene.'

Lily offered up handshakes. 'Hello, I'm Lily. What brings you to this windswept part of England?'

'We got bored with London,' answered Irene. 'There were no English people there. So we hired a car and ended up here.'

'Oh, you're staying in our B&B, I recognise you now.'

'Yes, that's us,' continued Irene. 'What a quaint place. I

want to move to England but Harrison has a car parts business, back home in Michigan. Anyway, we're disturbing you...'

'No, no, I try to get up every fifteen minutes, or I feel I might stay down there forever. I'm glad you're having a great time.'

Harrison and Irene began to move away.

'You have a nice day,' said Harrison.

'You, too. See you soon.'


The Ford Fiesta made it to Sheffield and drove into the city centre, approaching and passing a *Welcome to Sheffield* sign.

'We should have shot the sign,' pointed out Dan.

'I agree, we should.'

Bodie directed Dan towards Anthony's address. They got lost once or twice before Dan pulled up in a bus stop and Bodie jogged over to the entranceway to a posh block of apartments. Bodie quickly came back and spoke to Dan through the open driver's window.

'No answer. He's not home.'

'So what now?' asked Dan.

Bodie jumped back in.

'We go see your family?' asked Dan.

'That's as good a plan as anything else.'

They got lost again, until Bodie recognised the way needed to navigate through the city centre. Entering the correct suburb, Bodie pointed to the Retirement Home building that he intended to visit. Dan dropped him at the car-park entrance, saying he was going for a coffee and would be back in an hour.

'Do you not want to come in and wait?' asked Bodie. 'There might be a Bridge game you can join in with.'

'Tempting... but no.'

Bodie entered reception and was greeted by the Retirement Home Manager, who introduced herself as Patricia. After briefly explaining the nature of his visit, Bodie allowed Patricia to lead him through to a communal television room. Bodie's grandparents looked up and waved at him, which satisfied Patricia, who went back to her office.

'Tom!' called his grandmother, Doreen. 'Hello, my darling.'

Grandfather, William, grinned at him. Bodie kissed them both, then sat beside them.

'Am I in time for bingo?' he asked.

'Oh, Tom, it's lovely to see you,' said Doreen.

'I thought it had been too long since I was here. How are you both?'

Doreen indicated William. 'Oh, he's a nuisance as always, but I wouldn't be without him. Are you still with that lovely girl?'

'Which girl would that be, Gran?' he teased.

They all laughed.

'What was her name?' Doreen tried to remember. 'Maria, that was it.'

'No, not with Maria, any more. I remember, she did your Sudoku with you, didn't she, when we came here. Are you both well, then?'

'We are,' said William. 'I get out to play bowls, twice a week. It's a nice place, this. We're very content. Are you staying for a brew?'

'Yes, definitely. Shall I organise it?'

Bodie stayed with his grandparents for an hour, having tea and being introduced to some of their friends. Then he promised to return soon, kissed them again, and went out in search of Dan. In a quiet part of reception, he paused to take a moment thinking about his grandparents, then took a deep breath and went outside, seeing Dan waiting for him.

'Are they well?' asked Dan.

'Yes, very cheery.'

'Where to now?'

'Do you know any florists?'

'Florists? Not off the top of my head.'

Dan found a florist from *Google* on his cell, drove them around to the shop, and Bodie bought some nice Carnations. Then Dan took them both to the nearby cemetery. He stayed at the car, while Bodie went in alone.

Bodie walked amongst the gravestones. There wasn't a soul about, just a noisy pair of crows. He soon found his way and stopped before a headstone which showed both the names of his parents: Martin and Lucy Bodie, who had died on the same day in 2015. Bodie squatted down in front of the stone and placed down the flowers. He tidied up around the grave a little bit. In his mind, he said hello to his mum and dad, and engaged them in conversation. Told them how much he missed them and that he could have done with them right then and there. He apologised for not bringing Lily to meet them.

He had a little cry. Then he straightened up, wiped his eyes, and went back out to Dan.

They decided to try Anthony's place again. Dan managed to find a parking spot, so they both walked to the entrance to the apartments. It had become dull and overcast, late in the day, and Dan was mumbling about being hungry. Bodie buzzed Anthony's number again.

Dan grumbled under his breath. 'This guy is so deep undercover that we can't find him.'

Then Bodie felt a finger jabbed into the middle of his back, like a gun barrel.

'What's your game?' asked a man's voice.

Bodie paused. 'I like a bit of snooker, now and again.' Then he spun around laughing, to embrace an equally cheerful Anthony. 'Hey, your beard's come along a treat!'

Anthony checked out his cousin. 'What brings you back from beautiful Liverpool? Is it girl trouble again?'

'It was you that brought me back. You're the cause of the trouble.'

'Ah, well, it can't be any worse than this crew I'm working on right now.' He looked Dan up and down. 'Who's this clown?'

Bodie did the introductions, although the two men had probably met years ago. Anthony invited them up to his apartment. Going up the stairs, Anthony put an arm over Bodie's shoulder. 'Go on, then, what's the big mystery?'

# 7

Lily had a plate of cod, chips and mushy peas for her evening meal, in the local pub in Wrangle. Rebecca did suggest that they share a tiramisu for dessert, but they both felt too full up. Lily engaged in the banter around the tables, but inside she was fairly keyed up; it had proved impossible to contact Bodie. She had started to fret, to worry, to wonder if he had actually finished with her. Seeing Rebecca smiling with each received text from her boyfriend added to Lily's chagrin.

Over coffee, they all moved to the pool table area where Kenny and Ben played a few games. From her position on a stool, Lily could watch Professor Siddiq and Mrs Dunwoody chatting with members of the Local History Society. They seemed settled in for the night, dulling Lily's mood even more.

Lily noticed that nice American couple dining in the pub, and shared friendly waves with them.

Between pool games, the boys played a silly game on the

dartboard; whatever you scored with six darts would be the age at which you died. Jack got 95. Kenny was happy with 87. Ben only got five darts to stay in the board and scored just 28, much to everyone's amusement.

'I've only got nine years left!' laughed Ben.

The boys then continued to play pool.

Samia moved to be beside Lily, drawing a smile from her.

'You're not going to do anything silly, are you?' asked Samia.

Lily looked at her friend. 'Like what, attempt to embarrass myself by playing pool?'

Samia nodded in the direction of Professor Siddiq. 'He's married, you know, Lily.'

'Girl, I'm worrying about my boyfriend, not the professor. He seems to have fallen off the edge of the world.'

'Oh? Really? Can you not call his family or something?'

'He hasn't got much family. Maybe he's just enjoying his freedom while I'm away. I'll try him again before I turn in tonight.'

'Yes, you do that.'

They watched Kenny celebrate winning a game with a fluke.

Samia sighed. 'We'll soon be back in Liverpool.'

Lily stole another look at Professor Siddiq. 'You know, he's not married. What he is, Samia... is unhappily married.'

The two girls fell about laughing.

Ben came over, wanting Samia to play him at pool. She politely refused, at first, but Lily helped to get her off her stool and propelled towards the pool table. Lily laughed and watched her friend chalking her tip like there was no tomorrow. Ben finished his coke and then remonstrated for Samia to get on with the game. Lily applauded as Samia potted two balls on her break-off shot. Ben showed mock despair at the fluke. Everyone was laughing.

Inevitably, Lily would be coerced into playing, despite pleading sporting incompetence. Kenny stepped over to get her, and she agreed, just as Professor Siddiq occupied the stool beside her.

'How are all my wonderful students?' asked Professor Siddiq. 'Having fun?'

Samia passed over her cue to Lily, who pretended to seek her advice on chalking the tip.

'I can't do the break!' protested Lily, laughing.

Kenny did the honour, smacking the balls everywhere, without sinking one. Lily moved to position. Her Bodie was brilliant at pool, but she felt awkward. She knew which ball to aim for and cued up. It was like watching a new-born foal trying to stand up for the first time.

'Woah! Woah!' called Professor Siddiq, moving to be at Lily's side. He was horrified with the shape of her bridge hand, and helped her spread her fingers to allow the cue to run smoothly. He was being perfectly upstanding, not touching her anywhere else, but the simple feel of his hand on top of hers turned her face bright red. She hoped people would think it was the warmth of the pub or the strain of being over the table. She was so disappointed when he let her go. She tried to concentrate, moving the cue back and forth, and played the shot. The plastic sound of the ball hitting the pocket brought great cheers from her friends, as well as a handsome smile and applause from the Professor.

Anthony Harper had gone a little pale. He, Bodie and Dan were sitting watching *Coronation Street*, simply because that had been on when Anthony casually put the TV on. They had coffee and some stale brioche rolls in front of them. Dan was manically scratching at a small patch of eczema on his left elbow. Bodie had just described his experiences, back in Liverpool.

'My cousin worked on *Coronation Street* once,' said Dan. 'As an Extra. He did a scene with that Alya character. He said she was lovely.'

Anthony was focussed on Bodie. 'My God, Bodie. My God.'

Dan pulled his sleeve down. 'My sentiments, exactly.'

Anthony leant forward, to speak more to Bodie. 'It's a good job this apartment isn't in my name. Bodie, mate, I'm sorry you had to go through that. Wow.'

'Who was the American sailor?' asked Bodie. 'That man, Dean?'

'He gave me a story recently, risking his career, about the US Navy harming sea life. He must have had something bigger for me. Much bigger.' Anthony rocked back and forth, rubbing his face, while he thought. 'Okay, okay, I've got contacts within the Chief Constable of Greater Manchester's office. First thing in the morning we could go there. We should have protection before I even try to expose this.'

'They tracked me by my cell phone. So, they know about Lily. I'm frightened for her. She's away with college at an archaeological dig in Lincolnshire. Anthony, you say we could go to the police? You're not definite?'

'I'm in two minds. If I just run for help, I probably lose the exclusivity on the story.'

Dan sat forward. 'And if you don't run for help, we could probably lose our lives.'

Anthony got up and paced about. 'Did Dean not say anything about what he wanted?'

Bodie shook his head. 'No. It all happened so quick.'

'Right, then, better to leave Lily alone. Why should they harm her?'

Bodie was being firm. 'Anthony, I need to get to her.'

Anthony stared at his cousin. 'Okay, okay, let's get to your girl, Lily. Then you two stay with her, somewhere safe, while I go for help.'

'Right,' said Bodie.

'Yay!' said Dan, clapping his hands together. 'Road trip.'


The following morning, Anthony did think about contacting his girlfriend, Anne-Marie, over in Woodseats - he had a deep urge to do that. And he did think about taking his BMW to Lincolnshire. But, in the end, he did neither, getting into the back of Dan's less than exciting vehicle. They stopped at a shopping area to pick up some snacks and soft drinks, and for Bodie to use a public telephone to call Lily.

'Don't warn her you are coming,' said Anthony. 'Just say you've been busy, blah, blah, blah.'

Bodie nodded. Anthony left him to it and moved over to where Dan stood. Dan passed him a newspaper.

'I've got some supplies,' said Dan. 'Are we ready to go, do

you reckon?'

'I think so.'

Anthony glanced at the newspaper, with a follow-up report on the mysterious deaths in Le Claire, Iowa.

'I so miss using my iPhone,' said Anthony. 'I suppose this newspaper will have to do for now. So, Danny Boy, what do you think of all this?'

Dan pulled on his goatee. 'I think it's totally crazy. I'm frightened, to be honest. But it's a buzz, too. Can you really sort it out?'

'I hope so. Let's get Lily safe, then take it from there. What about you, anyone you want to call?'

Dan thought of his mother. 'A girlfriend? Not at the moment. You?'

'I've got someone. But it's a bit... fluid, right now. She'll be okay. Look, Bodie's finished. Let's hit the road.'

At that very moment, back at Anthony's flat, Henry, the boss of the people smuggling ring, stepped from a Toyota Land Cruiser, together with two heavies, who were carrying sledge hammers. Henry, with a large blade tucked inside his leather jacket, had a steely, cold-blooded look on his face. Still, he paused, to check the weather. 'There may be rain.' One of the heavies nodded in agreement.

Anthony's cover had been blown and the man was to be dealt with in the most severe way possible. Henry strode across the pavement, as if he owned the place, then indicated for the heavies to gain him entry to the building, which they duly set about doing with aggressive gusto. Out came Henry's camera, to record the event from start to finish.

# 8

Margaret and Barry Fallon had both recently retired, after forty years of working; she as a nurse and, lately, a ward sister, and he as a car breakdown mechanic. They had brought up three wonderful children in that time, scrimping and saving to be able to give them the life that they themselves had not had. They owned their own semi-detached home in Bristol, drove a six-year-old Ford Mondeo, and holidayed every two years, either in a caravan at Weston-Super-Mare or a little hotel in Minehead, which were both on the Somerset coast. So, Margaret had decided to cash in a Life policy and get them both away on a proper holiday, for a change, and what was better than a world cruise? They were always being advertised on the television as amazing experiences, forty-three ports, all food included, cabaret, cinema, swimming pool, etc, etc.

Margaret was perhaps a little overweight, thick in the ankles and ruddy in the face. Barry was sinewy and a bit grizzled, with permanent black under his fingernails from decades of working under a bonnet. But they were in new holiday clothes, Margaret had a new perm, they were happy and enjoying themselves enormously. Margaret stood on one of the forward decks, waiting for Barry to return from the buffet. She thought back to their two stops, so far: to the island of Malta in the middle of the Mediterranean, and then Port Said, and to the formal meals enjoyed since leaving Southampton, four days previously. She thought ahead to all the marvellous places yet to visit: Mumbai, Singapore, Sydney, Auckland, to name but a few, and they had already made new friends around ship. In fact, Janet and Frank, a younger couple from Exeter, were approaching her. *Where was Barry?* No doubt, he would embarrass her by showing up with an overloaded plate of ham and sausages. Janet and Frank had to negotiate many fellow passengers, as the ship was just entering the Suez canal, which was an exciting spectacle.

'Margaret! Hello!' called Janet.

'Hellooo! Isn't this great? The famous Suez canal.'

Frank leant on the rail. 'Oh, you've got a good spot here, Margaret.' He was wearing a floppy white hat, bought at the Wimbledon tennis championships that year, and was carrying his expensive camera.

'Where's Barry?' asked Janet.

Margaret rolled her eyes. 'He can't stay away from the buffet table. He thinks that because it's free he has to make the most of it. Silly man.'

Janet laughed, indicating her husband. 'He's much the same.'

'Not too hot, is it?'

'No, no, I was expecting much worse. Wait 'til we get further east. Oh, here's Barry now.'

A smiling Barry joined them. Margaret forgave him because he was only carrying a plate of sandwiches. He squeezed in between his wife and Janet and looked out at the view.

'So, this is the famous Suez canal?' said Barry, stuffing his face.

'Look,' said Janet, 'Some locals, waving at the ship.'

Frank started to film the view.

Six hours later, in Teddington, south west London, nineteen-year-old Maria Cowfield was watching television news.

'Muuuum! Come and see this!'

Mrs Cowfield rushed in from the kitchen, thinking the neighbours were fighting naked in the street again. 'What on earth is it!?'

'You're not going on that cruise.'

'Oh, well, tell your father, so he can stop packing. What's wrong, anyway?'

'Just watch this.'

Amateur camerawork showed passengers on the deck of a cruise ship. The caption below read: Suez Canal.

'We're not going anywhere near the Suez canal,' pointed out Mrs Cowfield.

'Shush!'

As the camera panned outwards it picked up a bright flash, followed by a white streak of smoke. Instantly there came the sound of an explosion and screaming. The camera started to shake a little, but filmed another swirling white trail, then another, with more thuds and screams, with passengers rushing away from the rail. "Oh my God, Barry," came a woman's voice, off camera. Then there were three more rockets fired at the ship, together with automatic gunfire. The camera filmed two members of ship security running to the rail with hand guns, trying to return fire. Then it went black. The TV news briefly returned to the two presenters, then the clip started on a loop.

'That's awful,' said Maria. 'They haven't said anything more yet, about casualties.'

'Oh, well. It's happened now, it's not likely to happen to me and your father.'

'Mother!'

'Especially in Norway.'

With that, Mrs Cowfield went back to cooking tea, and Maria decided to go for a shower, before work.

Professor Siddiq was in the farmhouse near to the dig, the place where all the information was gathered together and finds were catalogued. A lady from Lincoln University got the news of the terrorist attack on the cruise ship up on her cell, and everyone crowded around to watch. There were gasps all round.

Disgusted, shaking his head in despair, Professor Siddiq stepped outside. A strong breeze moved over his face - he needed it. It was getting a bit stormy. He looked across to where his people were. They were leaving later that evening, missing the traffic. It had been a fun experience, but now he wondered if all the things he was to live through for the rest of his life would be tainted by the backdrop of constant upheaval and violence in the world. He sighed deeply.

'Professor!' shouted Lily, waving him over. 'Come and see what I've found.'

He hurried over, everyone smiling at him. A member of the Local History Society passed him a coin which he had been examining.

'I'm told it's a sestertius,' said Lily, grinning from ear to ear.

Professor Siddiq smiled warmly and patted her on the arm. 'Well done, Lily. Well done.'

Lily blushed. 'Thank you, Professor.'

Professor Siddiq looked at Lily. She wore a bandana, but some of her wild black hair was blowing in the wind. Her smile was still broad, her teeth perfect. She really was such a pretty girl. If she were only a few years older, and not a student... He shook the ridiculous thought from his head and gave her a friendly punch to the shoulder. 'On the last day, as well. Way to go, you.'

'I know, I'm so pleased.'

Professor Siddiq clapped his hands together. 'Well, everyone, finish your assignments, we'll be packing up in a few hours.'

Everyone drifted back to the trenches. Professor Siddiq pulled out his trowel and jumped in beside the three boys.

'*Andrew Page!*' shouted Dan, from the passenger seat.

It disturbed Anthony, who was lolling in the back seat. 'What!? Andrew who!?'

Bodie just laughed, taking his turn behind the driving wheel.

'An *Andrew Page* delivery van. I always shout out when I see a firm that one of my relatives works for.'

'Oh, good God,' despaired Anthony, sitting up. He let out a long yawn. 'Where are we, exactly?'

'We're coming into a place called Horncastle,' answered Bodie. 'Well inside Lincolnshire now.'

'*Hermes!*' shouted Dan.

Dan and Bodie laughed their heads off.

Bodie parked in a bay, on a row of shops. They all got out and looked about the pretty, old town. There were lots of shoppers milling around.

'Oh, I'll pay the parking, then,' joked Dan, going to a Pay & Display machine.

'Horncastle,' said Bodie. 'Pretty place.'

Bodie saw restaurants, shoe shops, a butchers, and a Fish & Chip shop that had some tables in. Anthony nodded when he indicated that they should go in there.

They took places by the window. Anthony ordered three haddock and chips and three cokes. Anthony took his newspaper out and showed them the Le Claire incident.

'Isn't that weird,' said Anthony. 'I just remembered that there was a similar thing happened on the Thames in Berkshire.'

Bodie and Dan nodded politely, then returned to watching

girls passing by the window.

'So?' asked Anthony. 'What's the plan for Lily? We can't just drive up to where she is, assuming she's being watched.'

That had their attention.

'Well, I'm a stranger,' said Dan, 'so I could go and speak to her, take her a note from Bodie.'

'That's possible, I suppose,' said Anthony. 'It might scare her, though. Bodie, did you say she's on an archaeological dig? What if we dress like scruffy students? But, Dan, you can stay as you are.'

Dan grinned at the joke.

Their food was served to them. They were all profusely polite to the nice serving lady. The salt and vinegar was passed around.

'Cycling,' said Dan.

'I beg your pardon?' asked Anthony.

'We hire some bikes. Get all the cycling gear on. We cycle past the dig and stop, by chance, to have a look.'

Bodie and Anthony exchanged looks, happy with that plan. They all pounced on their meals.

# 9

Professor Siddiq stood with Lily and the other students in front of their mini-bus, drinking tea.

'So, our last day here,' the Professor said to Lily. 'I think it's been an exceptionally positive expedition. Lots to keep us busy for a while when we get back to Merseyside.'

'I'm surprised Mrs Siddiq didn't pay us a visit, like she did at Carlisle.'

'She's a bit busy, opening another surgery. Bringing her form of dental torture to the good people of Wallasey.'

Lily giggled.

'Is your boyfriend waiting for you, Lily?'

'I do hope so.'

Professor Siddiq scanned the sky. 'Well, we've been lucky

with the weather. Looks like rain moving in now, though.'

'Professor Siddiq, I wanted to thank you for letting me come along again. I really had fun out here.'

'Oh, Lily, it wouldn't be a dig without having you with us.'

He gave Lily a little hug.

Bodie, Anthony and Dan were cycling along in torrential rain. There was absolutely no shelter for miles around. They passed an ornate sign at the side of the road: Old Leake.

'Fantastic idea of yours, Dan,' called Anthony, with heavy sarcasm.

They rode on, and on. The rain seemed to move in at them horizontally. Eventually, the three cyclists approached a church, with nearby houses.

'The lych gate,' shouted Bodie. 'Let's get under there.'

They rolled to a stop and sheltered under the small, wooden lych gate. They were like three drowned rats.

A vicar, under his umbrella, walked nearby. 'Hello, gentlemen! Terrible day for it.'

Anthony laughed and waved. 'Could you tell us where the archaeological dig is taking place, please?'

'You can see it there, my friends, where that school bus is.'

They all looked through the rain to where the vicar had indicated.

'Thank you!' called Anthony.

Professor Siddiq and the students were drenched, as they hurried to pack the mini-bus. Lily laughed and apologised as she bumped into Jack.

'Hurry, everyone,' called Professor Siddiq. 'We'll get back to the B&B and regroup, before the journey home.'

Lily apologised as she bumped into someone else. But that someone held onto her. She was shocked and cried out a little, until she recognised Bodie's face. She was astonished to see him there.

'Lily, it's me, Bodie. It's all right.'

'Bodie! What on earth!?'

Before Bodie could say another word he was rugby-tackled to the soaking turf by Professor Siddiq. Lily squealed and rushed to the wrestling pair.

'Professor! Professor!' shouted Lily, 'it's all right. It's my boyfriend! It's my boyfriend!'

Professor Siddiq knelt up off Bodie. 'Your boyfriend, Lily!? I thought you were being attacked. Good grief!'

Lily welled up at the thought that Professor Siddiq would rush to her aid. They all stood up. Lily stared at her boyfriend, wanting to know why he was there. And why he was dressed like a Tour de France cyclist.

Professor Siddiq was not at all happy with Bodie. 'You should have given us notice of your intended visit.'

'Yes, I'm sorry.'

Lily made an attempt at normalising the situation. 'Bodie, this is Professor Siddiq. You remember me telling you about him?'

'Oh, yeah.'

Bizarrely, in a rainy field in Lincolnshire, Bodie and Professor Siddiq shook hands.

'Nice to meet you,' said Bodie.

'Bodie? From the 80's detective show?'

'No.' Slightly annoyed to hear that one yet again, Bodie turned to Lily. 'We have to talk.'

'Come back to the B&B,' said Lily.

'We have to talk *now*, babe.'

Bodie and Lily stepped to the side. But before they could talk, Harrison and Irene, the two Americans from the B&B, were standing there.

'What's your name, son?' Harrison asked of Bodie.

Bodie declined to speak. Harrison threatened him with a hand gun.

'I asked you your name?'

Dan suddenly appeared out of the gloom, pressing his gun against Irene's head. Immediately after, Anthony, back in thug mode, relieved Harrison and Irene of their guns. Professor Siddiq, Mrs Dunwoody and the other students stood looking on, flabbergasted.

Professor Siddiq felt that he should intervene. 'I want to know what is happening here!?'

Anthony gave one gun to Bodie, keeping the other for himself.

Dan turned to Professor Siddiq. 'Keys to the van, please.'

'Certainly not!'

Harrison and Irene took their chance and made a hasty retreat, gambling that the civilians would not shoot them in the back. Dan pointed his gun at Professor Siddiq. Lily cried out.

'No. Don't,' said Lily.

'Get in and drive,' Dan threatened Professor Siddiq.

Under duress, Professor Siddiq got behind the wheel of the mini-bus. Dan was beside him, poking his gun into his side. Bodie, Lily and Anthony piled in the back, slammed the door, and the vehicle lumbered off into the rain. Professor Siddiq protested under his breath, and Lily was fairly traumatised. Bodie tried to hold her as the mini-bus rocked and bounced, seeking out the road.

'Lily, shush,' said Bodie. 'I'll explain everything. We just have to get away from this place.'

Harrison and Irene had run to their vehicle, where they had extracted their spare weapons from the glove compartment. Quickly, with Harrison driving, they set off in pursuit of the mini-bus.

Professor Siddiq found the road, and the mini-bus splashed along. The rain had suddenly stopped, but it was still very dark. They passed the other side of the Old Leake village sign.

'Where are we?' demanded Dan.

'Old Leake,' replied Professor Siddiq.

'Where does that take us?'

'Boston.'

'That'll do. Keep going.'

Anthony glanced back. 'We're being followed!'

Everyone either looked over a shoulder, or checked a rear-view mirror. Professor Siddiq started to object again, but Dan pressed the gun harder into his ribs and urged him on. The mini-bus rushed forward, the wipers going fast, even though it was not raining. Professor Siddiq gripped the wheel and stared right ahead. The mini-bus approached a bend. It took the turn but skidded slightly, kicked up mud, corrected itself, then skidded again on standing water. Almost in slow motion, it aquaplaned for fifty feet, across a junction, luckily as nothing was coming, and came to a stop with a thud against the left wall of a small bridge. Harrison's car took the bend too fast and he skidded left, then right, coming to a stop, side on to the crashed mini-bus. Harrison got out of the car and fired several shots into the mini-bus, shattering windows. Lily screamed at the sound of the exploding windows, as Bodie covered her with his body.

'Out, Lily! Out!' shouted Bodie, pulling his girlfriend from the mini-bus, as two more shots thudded into a side panel with metallic pings.

Anthony was first to return fire. Dan jumped behind the stonework and fired a volley of shots into the American's car. Irene was shooting. Bodie, keeping Lily on the ground beneath him, fired a couple of shots, hitting Irene in the right foot. It was pure luck, but was enough to give a pause to the shooting.

Harrison scrambled over to check on his wounded, cursing colleague, before shooting again. Bodie opened up, in reply, hitting Harrison in the left arm.

With both Harrison and Irene immobilised, Bodie's group clambered back into the mini-bus and Dan got behind the wheel. With a crunch of gears, and a few swear words, he backed it off the wall and drove them away at speed.

Dan was completely elated at the gun action. 'Wow! What was that!? That, people, was the gunfight at the Old Leake canal.'

Professor Siddiq was hanging on in the front passenger seat, aghast at Dan. 'I think you'll find it's called a drainage ditch, round these parts.'

'Hey, don't spoil it, man! Gunfight at the Old Leake canal!'

Lily was staring at Dan. He mimed a "what!?"

'What are you talking about?' she asked.

'Gunfight at the Old Leake Canal. Gunfight at the OK Corral.'

'I don't get it.'

'Wyatt Earp? Doc Holliday?'

Lily shook her head, none the wiser. 'No.'

'Oh, come on..?' despaired Dan, laughing.

Dan saw a road sign for Lincoln, so headed there, instead of Boston. It didn't take too long to get there. In a side street, they intended to abandon the bullet-ridden mini-bus. Luckily, there were two jackets in the vehicle, so Professor Siddiq and Bodie could at least hide their mud-soaked clothing, following their wrestling match.

The group walked on into the historic city. Professor Siddiq insisted on taking charge of Lily, in his teacher/pupil capacity, so Bodie was demoted to walking at the back of the group. Lily looked back at him a couple of times, grinning.

An adrenalin rush had just started to dissipate within Bodie, although his hands still trembled - he had just been involved in an exchange of gunfire with operatives of some shadowy government agency, and it was insanely scary. Plus, he was also very cold after getting soaked through, earlier.

Luckily, Anthony took them into the first pub they came to, and they all ordered coffee or tea, in the snug area. Dan apologised to Professor Siddiq for his aggressive behaviour, they shook hands, and both sat there talking quietly. Lily moved to sit beside Bodie, holding his hand. Anthony took charge, slowly explaining to Lily and the Professor exactly what was going on. Lily's eyes went wide and she was devastated to hear what Bodie had been through, while Professor Siddiq sat in silence, taking it all in. He had thought the whole thing had been a simple case of crime and abduction, like bank robbers taking hostages. But then it all made more sense and, although he was perplexed and disturbed, he accepted the situation.

'So, what should I do now?' asked Professor Siddiq.

Lily asked Bodie, 'Can we not go to the police?'

Bodie hugged her. 'Well, we think we need to go higher than the police. Anthony has connections. That's why we want to lie low while he goes. But, the Professor here, he has family who will be worried for him.'

'Shall we stay here?' asked Dan. 'They've got rooms available in the *Travelodge*, next door.'

Anthony looked at Professor Siddiq. 'Well, Professor?'

'I don't pretend to understand why something so extreme is happening here. But I could go to the police in complete ignorance, apart from the violent events of the day. I won't tell them where you are. I'll just say you dumped me at the side of the road. On the other hand, I am loath to leave Lily. I'm responsible for her. Yes, Bodie, I know you are the young lady's boyfriend, but in the eyes of the law Lily signed up for my expedition. I feel I should stay. At least until Anthony here has made attempts to contact the correct people.'

'But your wife, Professor?' said Lily.

'Thank you, Lily, but my wife is a tough character. She'll be secretly delighted with my kidnapping at gunpoint.'

Dan laughed at that, then apologised with a raised hand.

'Okay, then,' said Anthony. 'We'll get rooms next door. First thing first, we need to buy some clothes, get out of these wet and muddy things. As for the hotel, we check in separately... well, Bodie with Lily, me and the Professor. Dan, you're Billy No Mates.'

'Always with the gags,' joked Dan, laughing.

# 10

Doctor Brian Rhodes had decided to accompany his wife, Vivienne, down to London from their home in Milton Keynes, Buckinghamshire. While she attended a food franchise conference at Earls Court, in relation to her catering company, he would do the tourist thing, before they would meet up at the hotel in the evening. Of course, all the recent terrorist attacks did concern him but, like boarding a plane immediately after another one had crashed, he felt safe at that particular moment.

On Tuesday, he had done the Tower of London, loving the tour with a bewhiskered Beefeater and seeing Anne Boleyn's memorial. He had taken a moment to imagine the famous lady's feelings as she was held in the Tower. Wednesday had been a ride on the London Eye and a visit to the Houses of Parliament.

Now, he was on the tour of Wembley stadium. It was the first tour of the day. The cleaners were still in, following a big match the night before, and now they were preparing the pitch for the first NFL game of the season, hoisting the uprights into place and marking out the pitch. He wondered if his Cleveland Browns were coming to town.

What an astonishing place, he thought. He was only thirty years old, so had never been to the old Wembley, had only ever seen it on television with re-runs of FA Cup finals and international matches. He would have preferred them to have incorporated the white domes of the twin towers, but the magnificent arch spanning the stadium was impressive enough. He looked up to the sky. It was suddenly very cloudy, and he could see an inspection pod moving very slowly down inside the arch (which was a surprise); two men on board, obviously running from the weather. He hoped it wouldn't disturb the NFL work.

Spots of rain hit his jacket, as well as the lenses of a dozen or so Japanese tourists, there with him. There was a school party, also, and they were getting into their coats. The Tour Guide told everyone not to worry, that they would be going inside to see the changing rooms, very soon.

Brian looked out across the grass, imagining himself turning out for England, being the No. 10, playing a one-two with Dele Alli, skipping through the Dutch defence, curling a shot in off the right hand post. The crowd going wild. A small grin formed on his face.

Suddenly, the sky seemed to fold in on the stadium, blackness and wild winds, noise and madness. Before he knew it, Brian was blown backwards into a group of screaming Japanese people, as if he were a bowling ball hitting pins. They all finished in a heap inside one of the holes in the ground which are used by match-day photographers. Light came and went, but the noise raged, and Brian, on top of the pile, could see that everyone else had simply gone - swept away. He couldn't move, held down by the force of the event. He made his mind keep working, and came to the conclusion that a tornado had hit Wembley stadium. A massive tornado, a malevolent monster, the like of which had never before been seen in London.

A huge whoosh moved over Brian, trying to suck the air from his body, causing him to mentally accept that his time was up. Then it was gone, allowing light to creep back in. He realised that he was covered in soil and grass, and when he wiped his face, the day seemed strangely normal again. Normal, except that the gorgeous green pitch had vanished, including all the workmen and the gridiron posts, and there was a gaping hole where the West stand should have been.

Brian climbed out of the hole and helped up the five Japanese men and one woman who had been beneath him. He told them he was a doctor and quickly checked them over, but there was nothing wrong with them, apart from shock. Two of the men quickly resumed their photograph taking. There was nobody else around, nobody at all, to receive Brian's medical attention.

He slowly looked up. To his complete and utter

astonishment, the famous Wembley arch was no longer there.

Bodie and Lily woke up entwined together on their hotel bed, both fully dressed in casual clothes that they had bought from a charity shop.

Bodie extricated his right arm from beneath her body and held the lifeless, floppy limb until the blood finally returned to it. It was an extremely unpleasant sensation, and he had to just sit there and yawn his way through it. Then, he went to do some ablutions.

Lily was awake when he returned to the bedroom, sitting up, her wild Indonesian hair making him grin with happiness.

'Hiya,' she said, smiling.

'Hello, you.'

She pulled a sulky face. 'I wanted to climb over you, to the bathroom, like a good English wife.'

He laughed. 'Is that what you think constitutes being a good English wife? Are you ready for some breakfast?'

'I am, yes. I'll have it in bed.'

'No, you won't, you cheeky mare. We'll go down to the restaurant.'

Bodie waited while his girlfriend showered. As the wait went on interminably, he switched on the TV, but on the news there was something crazy going on with the weather, so he channel-hopped, finding sub-humans shouting at each other over a paternity test on ITV Daytime; UK Gold was showing *Top Gear* in Romania, yet again, and there was ski-jumping without any snow on Eurosport, so he turned it off.

Lily finally reappeared, all groomed and fresh.

'Mrs Bodie, you look ravishing.'

'Why, thank you, Mr Bodie.'

They wandered down to the restaurant for breakfast. Amongst several holidaying families, Anthony and Professor Siddiq sat there, looking like *The Odd Couple*. They ignored them and found a free table.

Professor Siddiq sipped his orange juice, jealous of Bodie for having breakfast with the adorable Lily, then returned his attention to Anthony. 'So, tell me, Anthony, what are you thinking?'

'I don't honestly know.'

'Perhaps you think it's all terrorist related?'

Anthony finished his scrambled eggs and pushed his plate away. 'Well, to kill the sailor, to try to kill Bodie, and us. It must be big. Perhaps I.S. terrorists are about to do something massive, and if the story comes out, it will cause mass panic.'

'You can't be suggesting they've got a nuclear weapon? Here, on UK soil?'

'Well, maybe a dirty bomb.'

'How could your American sailor friend know about it? Unless it's coming in by ship.'

'London? Up the Thames? There were those strange deaths, higher up the river.'

'I saw that. But there was something similar in America. And in Jakarta.'

'Jakarta? I didn't know about that.'

'Yes. People dead in the street. Like a plague.'

Anthony sat up straight. 'Plague? Professor, that's a bad word.'

They got to their feet and wandered through to reception. They took seats, waiting patiently on the others. There was only one receptionist on, with a big TV above her head, showing the news. The Prime Minister appeared on screen. The banner running along the bottom described his visit to the Isle of Wight.

'What's that all about?' asked Anthony, pointing to the screen.

'They built that eco-village on the Isle of Wight.'

'Eco-village?'

'A huge, air-conditioned bubble. With a controlled atmosphere, and all that involves. It's a private enterprise by one of those dot.com billionaires, and it's all highly secretive.'

'Why's the Prime Minister going there if we have this terrorist thing about to happen?'

They just looked at each other.

Dan appeared first, having decided to give breakfast a miss. He was wearing second-hand jeans and a pale *Firetrap* top, which had cost Anthony the princely sum of £4.50. He slouched down in one of the leather arm chairs and looked at Anthony and Professor Siddiq. They all politely said good morning, as if they were strangers.

When Bodie and Lily came through, fifteen minutes later, Dan got up and moved about the foyer, although he stayed within listening distance.

'I believe that we are near to Lincoln Library,' said Professor Siddiq. 'I wish to call my wife, just to reassure her.'

'We need to call Lily's brother, as well,' said Bodie.

Professor Siddiq nodded. 'Yes. And while there I want to

look something up on the internet.'

They took two taxis to the library. Bodie and Lily, holding hands, followed Anthony and the Professor inside, with Dan bringing up the rear. The telephone calls were made, before they gathered together in a seating area, near to the main entrance.

'Well?' Anthony asked of Lily.

'He's very upset and worried, but trusts me, for now.'

Professor Siddiq smiled at Lily. 'My wife threatened divorce if I don't return immediately. She's a little highly strung. Anthony, would you accompany me to the computer section, please?'

'Of course, Professor.'

Dan made himself comfortable. 'We'll be right here.'

Anthony and Professor Siddiq sought out the help of a Librarian and were soon settled at a computer terminal. First, they looked at all the unexplained mass deaths around the world, and all the speculation and conspiracy theories over the causes. Then they *Googled* the US Naval Fleet, discovering that it was spread out around the globe. The official line was that they were on international goodwill tours.

'Well, I'm none the wiser,' said Anthony.

Professor Siddiq just made a humming sound in his throat.

'So, what do we do now?' asked Anthony. 'Just run for official help?'

'Something's bothering me, Anthony. But I don't know what.'

'We can't remain on the run. Our thoughts were to get Lily. Well, we have her. I'll catch a train for Manchester tonight.'

The Professor leant back in his chair, running fingers through his hair. 'I have a tremendous urge to run to my wife. But also that I don't have enough time to do it.'

'You're puzzling me, Professor.'

'You're a reporter, you must sense something very wrong here?'

'I do, believe me. But we're being shot at. I'm not on the staff of the *Washington Post*, you know.'

'I just feel we should wait a little while before giving ourselves up. Maybe I should take the train, rush to my wife and try to bring her back with me?'

Then Anthony sighed back into his chair. He thought about collecting Anne-Marie in Sheffield, but she had a very small child. 'I suppose a couple more days won't matter.'

'Let's go and talk to the others.'

Bodie and Lily were snuggled up together.

'Lincoln is beautiful,' said Lily. 'I had the chance to study here. But chose Liverpool.'

Bodie teased, 'And what a wise decision that was.'

'I met you, didn't I?'

Bodie grinned. 'True. Kiss kiss?'

They kissed, pausing only as Anthony and the Professor approached, sitting themselves down.

'What's wrong, Professor?' asked Lily.

'I'm not quite sure, my dear. I'm really not sure.'

'The Professor wants us to wait before I seek help,' said Anthony. 'He thinks something will develop. Meanwhile, he wants to go home to collect his wife.'

'Why don't we go on to Lily's family in Newbury?' asked

Bodie. 'You can meet us there, Professor.'

Professor Siddiq shook his head. 'No, better if you stay here. Let's not complicate things. I'll be with my wife tonight and we'll come back on the next train.'

'Just like that?' asked Dan.

'She's a good wife, underneath her bluster.'

Dan shrugged. 'Well, I don't mind chilling in Lincoln for a few more days.'

Bodie had a question for the Professor. 'And once you are back with your wife, if nothing's happened, Anthony goes to the authorities.'

'Yes, that's right.'

While Anthony took Professor Siddiq to the railway station, and Dan went back to the hotel for a snooze, Bodie and Lily walked, arm in arm, through Lincoln town centre.

Lily dropped her cheek to his left shoulder. 'This is like when we went to Lake Windermere. That was a lovely day.'

'Yes, wasn't it, baby? I liked Lake Coniston, too.'

Lily giggled. 'But we gave up looking for Lake Coniston.'

'Yes, but we had fun in the car, before we set off for home.'

'Thank you for coming to rescue me.'

'Don't mention it. I had to come for you, it was my duty. Are you surprised?'

'Well... a little. We've only been dating a few months, after all.'

'I guess I'm just an all-round nice guy.'

'You certainly are. Hey, I like our hotel room. Two more nights together.'

'Well, two more nights together, but in a different hotel.'

'Oh, why?'

'When the Professor gets back , we intend to meet him at the railway station. We don't want him bringing the bad people with him to the old hotel.'

'I understand.'

'Come on, let's get some coffee.'

Lily smiled and snuggled into him more.

'Your turn to buy,' joked Bodie.

Lily laughed, but fetched out her purse from her bag. In doing so, she dropped a scarf without realising. Two passing teenage men stopped to alert her, but they inadvertently invaded the space of the naturally nervous Bodie. Lily realised instantly that the two men were just being nice, but Bodie had already swivelled on his heels and punched both men at the same time, in a pincer movement. It was only enough to stun the men, and to enrage them at such an unprovoked attack. While they were still thinking about retaliation, Bodie kneed one in the groin and attempted to punch the other again. Lily was desperately trying to restrain her boyfriend, but the red mist had descended. Both men were up for the fight, by then, trying to punch Bodie in the head.

'Run, Lily!' shouted Bodie. 'Get out of it!'

'Bodie, it's all right!'

The melee spread across the pavement, with Bodie being punched and dragged down, and Lily being thrown about like a rag doll. Shoppers were shouting for them to stop. Younger onlookers, as expected, were filming the scene on their phones. Finally, Bodie managed to hurt one of the men so badly that he decided to roll up in a ball. That allowed Bodie to get the other man in a choke hold around the throat. Bodie was still trying to make Lily run for her life, and she was still trying to tell him that it was all a misunderstanding.

A male passerby stepped in and tried to make a citizens' arrest of Bodie, kneeling behind him and attempting to force an arm up his back. Lily was not having that! She hurled herself at the man, hitting his face and scratching for his eyes. She was a wildcat. The man got up and tried to back away, faced with the fury of the Indonesian girl. She slapped him again and screamed abuse at him in her native tongue.

Bodie, a bit bloodied and exhausted, just got to his feet and admired his amazing Lily. As she went to slap the man again, Bodie grabbed her by the waist, picked her up easily, and put her down safely away from everyone. Then they fled through the shopping area.

# 11

Maria Cowfield, from Teddington, decided to go to the shopping mall on her own. Her friends had called, trying to make her go out with them, but she needed to be alone; she had things to think through, and she did that best while engaging in retail therapy.

The problem was: her boyfriend, Johnny. After a good first few months together, he was displaying classic signs of wanting more freedom, wanting to be back with the boys; being attentive one minute, and moody the next. In other words: he wanted to be a nineteen-year-old London boy, free to cop off at will, go to parties, and not be tied down to one woman.

Maria was very strong-minded. She felt that she loved

Johnny, that he was so cute, but she was smart enough to know when something was inevitable. She bought new jeans from *River Island*, and a set of polar bear pyjamas from *New Look*. She decided to find a coffee shop, where she could decide how best to let Johnny have his cake and eat it. She was wise beyond her years, knowing it was better to let him have his fun, rather than make it all heavy, and lose him completely. Who knows, she could always get rid of him herself, if she found someone else in the near future.

She enjoyed her coffee, while checking her messages. She thought about her college project. She checked out another customer's great hairstyle. She glanced again at the cute barista. Then she decided to get home; her parents had left that morning for their Scandinavian cruise, but there was Granny living with them, so she had to get back to make their tea.

At the door, not being very good at directions, she paused to remember where the best exit from the mall was. In front of her, there was a seating area, busy with a lot of people. Suddenly, in a great whoosh, these groups of tables seemed to go up with a smashing of crockery, coffee spewing everywhere, bodies displaced, screaming and confusion. It had only been a fraction of a second but it seemed to happen in slow motion before Maria's eyes. The screaming intensified, people were rushing about in her peripheral vision. Mangled and bloody bodies lay sprawled out of the concourse. She realised that everything had gone flying up because something had come flying down; or, more precisely, someone had come flying down, all the way from the top tier of the atrium.

Maria's heart was out of her chest. Her brain froze. But then she gathered herself, made herself understand that a man had fallen from a great height and landed on a group of ladies. Two women and the man were dead in front of her, being covered over by staff from a nearby bakery. She went to help another woman, whose leg seemed to be broken. She was splattered in coffee and blood, crying out in pain. Maria held her head in her lap and reassured her that help was on its way. People were rushing around. There was lots of shock and crying, but instantly all the injured women were being comforted, or treated, and within a minute the mall's medical team were there.

'Deliberate!' someone was saying. 'I saw him step up on the railing and fall forward. Oh my God!'

'I watched him, too,' said a horrified woman. 'It was awful.'

Maria handed her victim over to a First Aid person, and stepped away. She walked out of the mall before the police arrived, not wanting to get involved. She was surprised at how calm she was taking it. Her first real experience of terrorism. She got on the bus for home. Only then did she realise that her front was covered with blood.

Maria got home, and immediately went up to change her clothes in her bedroom. Then she checked on her Gran, in the lounge. Eighty-year-old, Rita Cowfield looked away from the TV and smiled at her granddaughter.

'Do you want a cup of tea, Gran?'

'That would be lovely, Maria. Did you buy anything nice?'

'Just a couple of things. Have you had a nice day?'

'Yes, dear.'

A repeat of *The Chase* quiz show was on the TV. Maria grinned as the presenter, Bradley Walsh, was laughing uncontrollably at a risqué question. Then she went to brew up. She had no intention of telling her Gran what she had just experienced. She wondered whether she would even tell her friends.

While she waited for the kettle to boil, Maria realised that her hands were trembling a little bit, but not too badly. Her cell vibrated beside her on the counter: Johnny. She just ignored it, wanting to be with her Gran. She took the tea through, and they sat there watching the end of the quiz. The team won £14,000, much to Mrs Cowfield's delight.

'I think they let them win, now and again,' said Maria.

'Oh, you and your conspiracy theories, dear.'

'The ratings require winners, Gran, now and again.'

Mrs Cowfield laughed, then channel-hopped. She had control of daytime TV, and the family had it in the evening. Maria was glad at some of the things her Gran skipped by, like *Last of the Summer Wine* and *Tipping Point*, then she settled on the BBC news.

There was Breaking News from Belgium. Grandmother and granddaughter watched as footage came in of a cycle race passing through a small Belgian town. An object falls from a building into the crowd of fans on the roadside. Maria gasped and put a hand to her mouth. The reporter was saying that it was a deliberate act to cause death and injury.

The Anchorman moved to other Breaking News, from a reporter in a Dusseldorf railway station. There was no camera-phone footage, but the banner at the bottom of the screen told of a man falling onto a group of commuters, that morning.

Suddenly feeling nauseous, Maria hurried from the room.

Bodie and Lily got back to the hotel, just as Anthony and Dan were checking out. Bodie had a blood-stained tissue pressed against his right eyebrow from a cut that wouldn't stop bleeding. At first, Anthony and Dan feared that the authorities had nearly captured him, but were then quite amused to hear the actual truth.

'That needs stitches,' said Anthony, being allowed a look at the wound.

Bodie grimaced. 'That's just super.'

'Let's get you two checked out of here,' continued Anthony. 'Then we'll get that cut seen to.'

Bodie and Lily gathered what few possessions they had in their room, and checked out of the hotel. The receptionist paid no attention to Bodie's facial injury, she probably saw much worse. She gave Anthony directions to the nearest hospital.

That turned out to be a short walk away. Dan spotted the red Accident & Emergency sign at the same time as Anthony pointed to a *Costa* coffee shop.

'We'll be in there, mate,' joked Dan to Bodie, slapping him on the shoulder. 'See you in six hours.'

Anthony guided Lily towards the coffee shop. 'You stay with him, Dan. I'm taking this beautiful, young woman for a coffee.'

Dan nodded. Bodie hugged Lily, then they separated.

The A&E department seemed relatively calm, with just half a dozen people sitting there waiting. While Bodie presented himself to the Triage nurse, Dan sat himself down. There was a TV on the wall. Dan nudged Bodie, as he sat down beside him. 'Look what's on, *Judge Rinder*. I love this show.'

Bodie crossed his ankles and settled in for the wait. After a few minutes, the two friends started chatting.

'Lily's a great girl,' said Dan.

'Yes, she is. She's amazing.'

'Tell me, has she got any sisters?'

'I think she does. If they come over, I'll be sure to fix you up. You'd be a right catch.'

Dan giggled, and stroked his goatee. 'Don't take your shirt off for the doctor.'

'Why not?'

'The small matter of the gun in your belt.'

'Oh, good point.'

'Wow, Bodie, man, I enjoyed that shooting in Old Leake. Given that nobody died, of course.'

'Only by pure chance.'

'I'm liking this holiday.'

'What about your courier job?'

'There are other firms. No worries.'

A male nurse, with a Scottish accent, had approached the waiting area. 'Mr Collins? Mr Collins?' Nobody moved.

'That'll be you,' grinned Dan, nudging Bodie.

Bodie stood up, remembering that he had given a false name. 'Sorry, I'm Collins. I was miles away.' He then went off with the nurse, pointing at his watch and saying to Dan, 'See, not a six hour wait.'

Bodie was cleaned up and given one staple above the eye.

He thanked the nurse and wandered back to Dan.

'Time for coffee,' said Dan, jumping to his feet.

They left by the same way they had gone in. An ambulance had just arrived and a serious casualty was about to be taken in. They lingered to watch. Dan casually looked around him, and happened to see, exiting the main hospital building, the American agent, Harrison. Harrison had his arm in a sling and was trying to get to his cigarettes in his breast pocket. He looked across and saw Dan staring at him. Neither men were totally 100% sure who they were looking at (if one or the other had glanced away it would have been missed) but something made them keep looking - maybe it was Harrison's trench coat, or Dan's hippy appearance. Anyway, the connection clicked into place and Harrison stopped reaching for his cigarettes and went for his gun, instead.

'Trouble, mate!' exclaimed Dan, making Bodie look.

'Hey!' shouted Harrison.

The American agent was perhaps fifty feet away, across two driveways and a wide flowerbed. He started to move towards them, pushing members of the public out of his way.

'Let's go!' said Bodie.

They bolted away, and both had to leap the stretcher case which was just exiting the ambulance, much to the paramedics' fury. By pure bad luck, two policemen were exiting their patrol car, forcing Bodie and Dan to detour back inside the hospital, with Harrison in pursuit.

A female nurse shouted at the two of them to stop running, so they slowed and hustled instead around several corners, trying to lose their pursuer. The American knew he couldn't chase them down, not in his condition, so he set about stalking the hospital corridors, trusting to chance.

Bodie and Dan entered the main building of the hospital. There was a plethora of departments to head towards, so Dan picked the yellow line on the floor and they rushed that way. They were almost intercepted by two hospital security guards, so dived left and ran along a corridor. A large nurse, hands on hips, blocked their way into X-Ray, so they took another turn. The security men were shouting for them to stop.

'A way out would be good!' gasped Dan.

They took a moment to breathe. That was when they spotted Harrison, through a glass wall, staring at them from an adjoining corridor. It was very frustrating for the American - he could have shot them dead, through the glass, but decided against such a shocking incident in a public place.

Bodie and Dan rushed on, finding an open window. Bodie went up onto the ledge like a cat. They were on the ground floor, but below the window the grass sloped away into a hollow. It was quite unnerving, but, with the security men only seconds behind, he flung himself out. He landed and tumbled forward down the slope, doing cartwheels. Dan followed immediately after him, landing slightly differently and sliding down the slope on his backside, shouting 'Youtube!!' Dan reached the bottom just as Bodie was getting to his feet, and took him down like ten-pins. Dan screamed with laughter. Then he got Bodie up again and the two of them hurried away.

# 12

Bulgarian, Daniel Berbatov, and Somali, Rageh Abdi, had a few things in common: both hated their sanctimonious, female boss, Karen, both despaired of the minimum wage, both hated the English, and both had only recently been given British citizenship.

Daniel was twenty years old, fairly handsome, despite a scraggly beard, while Rageh, nineteen, was clean shaven, with sharp features. Both worked at their local supermarket in Colchester, Essex. Daniel was usually a shelf-stacker, while Rageh was an order picker, collecting goods for home deliveries, although he wanted the Government to pay for driving lessons, so that he could get on the delivery vans. The two young men had been housed in neighbouring flats, and become friends. Daniel had a car (untaxed and uninsured) and he drove them both to work, each morning.

Although they had their issues, both men were fairly happy with life, and got along with their colleagues, as most were not English, anyway. They worked hard, and played five-a-side football together, when they weren't trying to meet girls. They liked computer games, playing *Call of Duty*, online. Daniel liked to cook, and often fed Rageh, in return for favourable comments. They watched movies together; usually big budget thrillers - Rageh liked the action. Rageh also liked conspiracy documentaries, from UFO's to 9/11. Recently, he had been bending his friend's ear about the big building project on the Isle of Wight, suggesting that it was a holding station for aliens. He was also constantly talking about the crazy weather; from the floods in Cumbria, to the mini-tsunami off the coast of Aberdeen, not to mention the catastrophe at Wembley. Daniel, although he looked fairly thuggish, with a scar under his left eye from a fight in an immigration centre, was quite a deep thinker. He listened to Rageh, weighed up the arguments, and usually came down on the global warming side, rather than the deliberate Governmental Pulse Weapon testing theory, which Rageh had suggested recently.

It was a Monday morning, suitably miserable in the supermarket. Karen, their boss, indulged in a team-building, rousing speech and group huddle on the back dock, which everyone immediately forgot. Then the deliveries started to arrive and the routine began, yet again, of stacking shelves and order picking.

Rageh had his stack of wheeled boxes with him, moving about, filling his orders while trying to avoid the nuisance that was shoppers, when he heard a disturbance in the next aisle. He walked around, seeing two female members of staff, Tina and Eva, together with Daniel. There were a great number of shoppers further along the aisle, near to the bottled water. Rageh sidled up alongside Daniel and watched as the shelves were stripped bare of bottles of mineral water. Then, the final few bottles were wrestled over by two men and a woman. The three people were sprawled on the floor, screaming obscenities, scratching and trying to throw punches. It was an astonishing sight - it was like *Black Friday* shopping for wide-screen TVs. Eventually, security staff reached the scene and tried to calm things down.

Karen, the manager, arrived alongside her staff, shaking her head.

'What's going on, Karen?' asked Tina.

'It's all over the news. There's a rumour out there that the water supply has been poisoned. By terrorists. The police have warned people not to drink tap water, while they do lab tests.'

'My God,' said Eva. 'Are we closing, then? Can we go home?'

'No, you can't. Get back to work. All of you. Slackers.'

Daniel walked away with Rageh.

'Could it be true?' asked Rageh. 'I hope so. Not for anyone to get hurt, just for the buzz.'

'If it's true, Rageh, it's crazy.'

'Come on, let's put our feet up in the staff room for a bit, while Karen is busy.'

They went into the tiny, window-less room, got coffee from the machine and slumped down on an old sofa, which was pock-marked with cigarette burns. Rageh took out his cell, to get the latest news.

'Why do you do that?' asked Daniel.

'Do what?'

'Obsess over the news. It's always grim.'

'Daniel, my friend, it's always fascinating. I tell you,

something big is happening.'

Daniel sipped his foul coffee. 'So you say, but you never show me any proof. An earthquake is coming... The army are doing a coup d'whatever... The world is coming to an end...'

'You'll apologise to me, one day.'

'Yeah, right.'

Rageh had read the news headlines. 'It's true about the water.'

'Good job I forgot to take my tablet this morning. I'd be dead now. I don't want to go that way.'

'What way do you want to go? Dying a slow, painful death after a car crash?'

'I don't want to go, at all.'

'The Prime Minister has called a Cobra meeting, while on the Isle of Wight.'

'A Cobra meeting? Oh, the emergency thing? So, they're all visiting your alien landing station.'

'I was reading people's opinions online, about that Isle of Wight thing, last night. It's...'

Karen appeared in the doorway. 'Out! Don't take the pee-pee. I'm too stressed to be chasing you two jokers today.'

Daniel and Rageh jumped up, and went back to work.

The police arrived to deal with the water "riots". Daniel and Rageh worked on, oblivious to it all. By lunchtime, the day had turned very sunny, so they ate sandwiches on a lawned area, out the back of the store. Daniel spent his half hour ogling the pretty check-out girl, Amanda, while Rageh stayed on his cell.

'Amanda has the prettiest smile I've ever seen,' mused Daniel. 'Pity she's dating Freddie, that English prick.' He threw the remains of his sandwich to a pigeon. 'Are you listening to me, Rageh?'

Rageh was a handsome guy, with light-brown skin and wide, smooth cheekbones. He had the whitest, best teeth in Essex, so he had taken a glance over at Amanda, but then returned to the raging torrent of views on the internet. His heart was beating faster. His mind was whirling - people were suggesting everything that Daniel had joked about earlier in the staff room. That the Government was evacuating London. Perhaps all the water in the country was about to be poisoned. Perhaps there were to be mass, co-ordinated terrorist attacks. The dirty bomb was mentioned.

Rageh finished his blackcurrant *Vimto* soft drink and picked up his cream cake dessert. Daniel was looking at him. Rageh loved a conspiracy, wanted something to happen to this lazy country, but he just could not decide whether to be frightened. Whether to go home after work, train for the five-a-side team, let Daniel cook dinner. Or whether to give in to the voice inside his head; the voice telling him to flee. Flee for his life. The same genetic urge that had made his father flee with him from Mogadishu, when he was only a child. Daniel was still looking at him.

'Are we going back to work?' asked Daniel. 'Or gambling that we win the lottery tonight?'

Rageh kept staring at his friend. 'Daniel, we have to go to the Isle of Wight.'

'S..sorry!?'

'We have to. We should ask your cousins to come with us. I want to ask my Dad, but I know he won't come, whatever I say.'

'Rageh, get a grip.'

'Daniel, we have to go, or we will die.'

Daniel felt a bit embarrassed, sensing other members of staff listening to Rageh's rant.

Karen came outside. Instantly, she focussed on Daniel and Rageh - they were not having a minute longer than company policy allowed. Daniel stood up as he spotted her, and pulled Rageh to his feet. Rageh was still being insistent, trying to make Daniel engage in eye contact with him, flicking at his arm with his hand.

'We have to,' said Rageh.

'Come on, mate, back to work.'

Karen was just in the action of looking at her watch, when Rageh rammed his cream cake right up her nose.

They went back to Daniel's apartment. Conversation was, not surprisingly, a little lacking. Daniel wondered if he was officially sacked, seeing as he had not actually attacked his manager with the cream cake.

Daniel automatically filled the kettle for a cup of tea, before Rageh reminded him of the current emergency. So they drank cans of *Dr Pepper* and sat on Daniel's tiny excuse for a balcony, watching the world go by. They had a view of a playground (that was never used), and a small row of dilapidated, graffiti-covered shops, where people kept coming and going, empty-handed, from the convenience store - clearly out of bottled water.

'Talk to me, then, Rageh.'

'The world is about to end, and the government are hiding away on the Isle of Wight.'

'Talk to me sensibly, Rageh.'

'Thirty-two,' said Joey Gulbis, sports correspondent for the *Kissimmee Daily Mail* newspaper. 'Thirty-three.'

Gulbis was the sole journalist covering the junior tennis competition, and beside him was the only photographer there: Mike Revell, a freelance. They were waiting for an up-and-coming junior player from Florida to compete, by the name of Annie Holden, a possible superstar of the future, but first they had to sit through a fairly tortuous match between two average twelve-year-old boys.

'Thirty four,' said Gulbis.

'What's with the count?' asked Revell.

'This kid from Orlando, he asks for the towel to wipe his face after every point. The poor ball girl spends more time running out with the towel than she does passing the ball. It should be stamped out, that kind of thing. It's.... crazy.'

'The kid clearly doesn't like to sweat.'

'Then he should take up chess. Thirty-five.'

The two journalistic friends watched the match stumble to a conclusion: 6-2, 6-2 to the boy who didn't mind sweating. The car-load of fans in the bleachers applauded.

More people arrived to watch the Annie Holden match; Gulbis estimated about seventy-five in total.

While they waited, Revell enquired after the health of Mrs Gulbis and kids, and Gulbis did likewise. Revell said that he hoped Holden won it quickly.

'Do you really believe the hype about her?' asked Gulbis.

'She's very strong for her age, with a killer backhand. Apparently, she has tennis-nut parents, with lots of dough behind them, so she will certainly make a good pro, if she wants it badly enough.'

'We certainly need some new blood coming through. No-one filled the void when the Williams sisters retired.'

Revell began taking pictures. 'Look, here she comes now.'

Gulbis recognised the tall girl, with a long blonde ponytail. Even from fifty feet away, her retainer was heavy duty. Her parents were her coaches, both sour-faced, both beside her as they settled to the left of the umpire chair. Annie's opponent was a recently arrived Serbian, called Natasha Panic. Gulbis hoped she also made it to the big time, simply because of her surname.

The interminably long time for a tennis match to begin, started with fluid intake, meeting the umpire, more fluid intake, intense coaching back at the chair, more fluid intake, then the knock-up, which tired out Gulbis simply by watching. Beside him, Revell clicked away.

'You might as well go now, Mike,' said Gulbis. 'You must have enough shots.'

'Ah, yes, but let's say our Annie girl twists an ankle in the third set, and I'm not here to capture it?'

'You're a pro.'

They were almost ready to play. Just some more fluid intake required.

'That's why they sweat so much,' said Revell.

Mimicking their adult tennis idols, both girls took their

towels to the back of the court and put them on a linesperson's chair.

From nowhere, a black storm moved across the Kissimmee area, right on top of the tennis club. Players, officials, parents, all stood about, taken totally by surprise.

'Where's this come from?' asked Gulbis, scanning the evil black cloud formation. 'It was supposed to be a clear day today.'

Boom!!! The thunder bounced both Gulbis and Revell off their seats. Everyone on the court was knocked flat. It had been the most terrifying, noisiest clap of thunder ever known by anyone present. It was stunning, stultifying, brain-numbing, dangerous; both players were out cold on the court, the umpire appeared to be having a heart attack, and Natasha Panic's elderly female coach, when people managed to gather their senses, would be found to be dead at the side of the court.

Revell recovered and began taking photos. Beside him, Gulbis surveyed the scene, with Mr and Mrs Holden staggering to their prone daughter. Gulbis began to write frantic copy.

# 13

In Liverpool, Professor Siddiq had taken a taxi from the Lime Street railway station, and paid it off a couple of streets from his house. He had then taken a circuitous walk, coming towards his house from the rear. There was a quick sprint over the darkened rear garden and then he was knocking on the back door until his surprised wife, Saba, let him in.

'Where have you been!?'

'Let me in.'

'Salman!'

Professor Siddiq had taken a sly look through the living room curtains, seeing a marked police car sitting there. Then he had turned to face his extremely distressed wife. What followed was the worst night of Saba Siddiq's life: anger, upset, confusion, palpitations, crying, until she fell asleep exhausted on the sofa.

Professor Siddiq napped in a chair, then made something to eat, at about 4 a.m. The police car was still there. He went back to the kitchen to wash his pots, watching the first glimmer of morning light over the rear willow trees.

Saba was standing there. Suddenly, she began trying to slap her husband's face, screaming at him. 'I'm not going! This is madness. What are you trying to do to us!? I hate you. I hate you.'

Professor Siddiq changed his clothes, collected some money and a few small personal items, one of which was a photo of his mother. Without another word to his sulking wife, he left the house the way he had arrived, and finally flagged down a black cab on the main road. Within the hour, he was back on a train to Lincolnshire.

He watched pensively as the countryside flashed by. Everything he had planned and worked towards was gone: the career, the reputation, the wife and family. He knew it was gone as he glanced across at two businessmen who were playing a game of travel chess. Professor Siddiq half-smiled to himself. On trains these days, people read books and newspapers, listened to music on their earphones (making everyone else listen to it, as well) or played with their cell phones; you almost never saw anything like two people playing chess. He looked at the pieces, positioned across the little wooden board. He stared so hard that his eyes lost focus, and he was almost completely sure of his conclusions.

Lily was taking a bubble bath, in their new hotel room. Bodie knew better than to try to get in with her, so he was sitting there at the end of the bath, massaging each little foot as she deemed to bring it out to him. He rubbed them, and forced the toes back, and told her she was far too tense, and she giggled like crazy.

'I'm very happy,' said Bodie. 'Even in these circumstances.'

'Sorry, what did you say?'

'I said I'm wearing a nappy, even in these cucumbers. Are you tired?'

'No, I was just thinking about the professor.'

'Would I be right in assuming you've got a little crush on our handsome academic?'

She giggled. 'Don't be silly, Bodie... It's a massive crush.'

They both laughed.

'Don't worry,' she assured him. 'I'm told it's quite normal to fancy a tutor. But I fancy you more.'

He pulled a face. 'Oh, good. That's all right, then.'

She flicked soap suds at him.

Professor Siddiq arrived at Lincoln Central Station and alighted from the carriage. In a world of his own, he headed towards the exit. By pure chance, he saw Bodie watching for him, standing on a far-off car park, away across all the tracks. He was about to wave, but saw Bodie's head turn slightly, looking behind him, along the platform. A quick check over his right shoulder proved that he had been followed from Liverpool; two big men in trench coats, moving after him. Shocked, he continued forward, amongst other passengers, livid with himself for being so careless, as well as being suddenly very frightened. He increased his pace slightly. He told himself not to look back again. He must not be taken! If he was correct in his summarisation, then he must not be taken.

Summoning up all his courage, taking deep breaths, Professor Siddiq leapt from the platform, landing in a heap, hoping not to have done himself an injury. People cried out in alarm. Cell phones were whipped out to film him, as a matter of course. Professor Siddiq got to his feet, and stumbled, scrambled, eventually ran towards Bodie. Bodie was waving and shouting encouragement, but all the blood pumping through his brain stopped him from hearing any sound. *Don't look back!* He knew he had enough distance between his chasers, even out of physical condition. He moved over the tracks, focussing on Bodie; on safety.

He could see that Bodie was behind a fence, and that made his heart sink. Was he to be grabbed and detained just before reaching safety. Bodie's face suddenly expressed horror and turned away! Why did he do that? A departing train missed Professor Siddiq by millimetres. The wash shook him to the core, and then the adrenalin rush was insane. Bodie turned back, white as a sheet, with a look of surprise that the Professor was still alive, and not a puddle on the ground. Then Bodie waved again. Professor Siddiq made the final push, up a grassy slope, to the fence, which turned out to be a flimsy, wire-mesh, and threw himself onto it. Bodie jumped forward and hauled the Professor over to the other side.

Professor Siddiq had one, despairing look back, at the two

agents who were following, but who were taking more care for their safety on the tracks, then Bodie was dragging him away from the station, and into a nearby housing estate.

Dan paused over his shot on the pool table. 'You know, I find it quite hard to play pool with a semi-automatic pistol stuck down the back of my undercrackers.'

'I have total sympathy for you,' said Bodie, chalking his cue.

They were in the games room of their new hotel, on the outskirts of Lincoln.

Dan giggled. 'I can't stop imagining the professor's face as that train went by him. Classic.'

Lily entered the room. Bodie smiled at her.

'How's the professor?' asked Bodie.

'Well, he took the food I offered him. But he's still very shaken up.'

'So, Mrs Siddiq wasn't such a good wife, after all,' said Dan, potting a ball.

Bodie hugged Lily. 'This has gone on long enough, baby. I'll speak to him later.'

Lily nodded, and snuggled in closer.

Soon, they joined Anthony for lunch. He was ready to put an end to it all, too. After their meals, they all went up to Professor Siddiq's room, and found him out on his balcony, with the wonderful backdrop of the iconic Lincoln Cathedral sitting on the horizon.

'Please, be seated,' offered Professor Siddiq. 'Do any of you play chess? No. But you are familiar with the idea of positioning your pieces before you attempt victory?'

They all nodded.

'I'm going to say something,' continued Professor Siddiq. 'It may be one of those occasions where a person has convinced himself of something, but it turns out that they are completely wrong. I hope this is one of those times.' He took a long look at the cathedral.

'The entire US Naval fleet is spread out across the globe, according to media reports. Apparently, they are on goodwill tours. One such ship is in Liverpool docks. A sailor from that vessel attempts to contact you, Anthony. Shadow forces, intelligence services, call them what you like, murder this sailor, and attempt to murder you, Bodie.' He looked at Lily. 'They put surveillance on you, Lily, following your phone contact with Bodie. Then they try to kill all of us at your gunfight at the Old Leake canal, Dan. Also, we have those reports of mysterious mass deaths. Without any explanation forthcoming. There was Berkshire, I believe, somewhere in Iowa, and Indonesia, that we know of. So, we have the chess pieces in position, we have sudden deaths, we have the conspiracy to silence anyone who might have an idea of what's happening. And we have the Prime Minister... with all his family, I saw on the news today, and all the Cabinet members, with their families, visiting this strange eco-village on the Isle of Wight, this coming weekend. Now, I cannot find other such projects in the news, but that doesn't mean they're not there.'

'Professor, what are you getting at?' asked Anthony.

'What I'm getting at, Anthony, is... I'm struggling to say it.'

Professor Siddiq looked tenderly at young Lily.

'The world is in an awful state,' continued the Professor.

'Don't you agree? Constant floods in Western Europe, perhaps from climate change. Famine in Africa, once more. Islamic State as strong as ever, making their attacks almost monthly now. The assassination of Prince William. I am rambling now, please forgive me. Too many people on the planet. Different religions. Horror everywhere. What I suggest. What I suggest... and I want to be proved ridiculous, is that those clever Americans are planning to release something into the atmosphere, something that has already leaked a bit - Berkshire, Iowa, Indonesia - something in the atmosphere to kill every human being on the planet who is not safely inside an air-conditioned environment. To... be rid of the horror. I don't know, maybe with the idea of starting again. Creating a new Garden of Eden. Once whatever this toxin is has dispersed, the survivors can come out and begin again. Imagine how quickly the earth would recover - rainforests, the climate, the pollution. No more terrorism, hunger or greed. A total, new beginning.'

Everyone just sat there and stared in astonishment at Professor Siddiq.

Lily went for a swim in the hotel pool; it was more of a doggy-paddle, as, back home in Surubaya, she never swam - she just wanted to try to relax her body and mind. Dan retreated to his room to listen to music, all afternoon. Bodie spent some time with Lily, then went for a walk on the grounds with Anthony, talking it through. The weather turned cloudy, bringing on an early dusk.

Later, Lily wanted some fresh air, so she and Bodie hugged,

sitting on the wall, out front of the hotel. Anthony came out and started to walk away.

'Anthony?' called Bodie, mildly concerned. 'Where are you going?'

'I'm going to find a payphone. I feel like calling my folks.'

'You're not going to tell them anything?'

'Of course not.'

Dan then came out.

'And where are you going?' asked Bodie.

'To get myself a *Big Mac* and a strawberry shake.'

Bodie watched both men go, then pulled Lily in tighter.

'Bodie, can he possibly be right about all that?' asked Lily. 'That's horrendous. Monstrous, I meant to say. My mind is shot to bits.'

'Shush. I don't know what to say, babe. There may be something in what he says. More than likely it's something to do with that. Like when we thought I.S. had a dirty bomb. That would scare enough people to cause a mass panic. Maybe that justifies what they're trying to do to us.'

'But the ships, Bodie? Spread out like that.'

'Maybe that's where the Prof becomes ridiculous. All a coincidence. Come back inside. Come on.'

Lily hopped off the wall, they embraced and went back inside the hotel.


Dan had taken directions from a receptionist on the front desk, found the nearest McDonald's restaurant and ordered his meal, sitting himself down to enjoy it. After a few minutes, he saw Anthony walk by the window, spot him, and came in to sit across the table from him.

'I'd recognise that beard anywhere,' joked Dan.

Anthony grinned. 'I was going to shave today, until Professor Siddiq hit us with both barrels. Tasty burger?'

'Good, yeah. Get one.'

'I'm watching my weight.'

They both laughed.

'We're both carrying hand guns,' said Dan. 'Can you believe that? Let's hold up the place.'

'And do what with the cash? According to the Professor, we die in four days time.'

Dan slurped up some milkshake.

'When I was a kid, I lived near Manchester airport,' said Anthony. 'I remember there was a news scare about terrorists hijacking small aircraft and spraying poison into the air. It really scared me. I didn't want to die like that.'

'Christ. Do you actually believe the Professor?'

'Yes.' He paused. 'Yes, I believe I do.'

'And what, if anything, can we do now?'

'We try to get into this eco-village thing on the Isle of Wight.'

'You know where the Isle of Wight is, right? It's an island, across that stretch of water off Southampton. It will be teeming with cops.'

Anthony ate some of Dan's fries. 'We can only try. All those migrants get across the Mediterranean. We only have to cross the Solent. Are you finished? Let's go get a beer.'

Dan binned his leftovers, but then went back to the serving counter. He bought a Happy Meal.

'What's that for?' asked Anthony.

Dan indicated that he would see. They stepped outside, walked across the precinct, where Dan squatted in front of a very young, female beggar. He left her with the meal, and then went for a drink with Anthony.

# 14

Wendy Webb rushed from her house, wearing just her pale blue nightie and large panda bear slippers. 'Hey! Hey! You!' She was a big woman and her bosom bounced wildly as she chased the Bin men and their noisy Refuse wagon, but she didn't care. It was certainly a sight for elderly Mr and Mrs Osmond, on their drive at No. 34, and an *Amazon* delivery man got an unwelcome eyeful, too. The bemused Bin men stopped what they were doing as she reached them.

Wendy, a heavy smoker, was out of breath. She took a moment to gather herself. She was red in the face. 'What do you think you're bloody doing!? You ignored my bin.'

'Your bin's overloaded, love,' answered a po-faced Bin man. 'Health and Safety, we can't take it.'

'Don't bloody Health and Safety me, you bloody jobsworth. And don't call me love. So, the lid's up a little bit.'

'Sorry, love.'

'Do you want my husband to come out and give you a smack in the face?'

'He can try, love.'

With that, the Bin men moved on. Wendy raged, turned on her heels, swore at the Osmonds, then gave a dirty look to the *Amazon* delivery man, 'What do you think you're looking at?'

She stormed back home, up her litter-strewn garden, past her husband, David's, stock car, which had its front wheels up on a ramp, and the family VW Camper van. She went in to her scruffy semi-detached and slammed her front door.

A few minutes later, Wendy's two teenage sons, Kirk and Steven, came out of the house. They picked up the bin, dumped the entire contents in the middle of the street, replaced the bin, and then got in their two old VW Golfs, which were parked on the road. With revving engines and wheel spins, they drove off to college.

Back in the Webb kitchen, David Webb was making his morning porridge. He wore tracksuit bottoms and a white tee-shirt with several different stains down the front. His salt and pepper hair was long over his ears, and he carried a double chin. His roll-up cigarette in his mouth dropped some ash in the porridge, but he did at least, very carefully, scoop it all out with a teaspoon before serving it up into a bowl. Wendy came in, putting the kettle on.

'Don't get so upset, sweetheart,' said David.

'I know, darling. But the lazy beggars really get my goat.'

David settled himself down with his *Daily Star* newspaper, guzzling his porridge. 'Look. Look at the headline. Water poison scare in Essex.'

Wendy put her cup of tea straight back down. The Webbs happened to live in a council house in Colchester, Essex.

'False alarm,' continued David. 'Tests prove negative.'

'Oh, that's all right, then.' She sat down to drink her tea. 'I thought you were telling me the world was ending again.'

'It is, sweetheart. Have no fear. You'll have to start believing me soon.'

'Can I have breakfast first?'

'There!' called David, pushing his bowl away, as he got to page two of his newspaper. 'All the buggers are on the Isle of Wight now. Oh my God, Wendy, something's going down.'

Wendy lit up a cigarette. She had had years of this kind of thing from her husband. The terrorist attacks had really set him off this last year, and the "Kamikaze" attacks, as the tabloids were calling the deliberate falls into groups of people, were the final straw. She herself was more concerned with the worsening weather events; the Wembley tornado had really frightened her. The odds were still massively against ever being involved in a terrorist attack. Secretly, though, she had read about the deaths on the Thames, and that seemed very strange to her. She looked at her husband. He had been on disability benefit for twelve years (although he handled a stock car well enough) and was usually quite laid-back. He was certainly spooked that morning.

'It's classic, Wendy. Oh, God, the poisoned water was supposed to happen. The government always flees before something catastrophic happens. They know! I tell you, they know!'

'Well, what if they do, darling? What are we supposed to do about it? Ring up Number Ten, Downing Street and ask for protection?'

David stared moodily at his wife. 'Where's my tea?'

Wendy huffed, but got up to make her husband a cup of tea. She plopped it down in front of him.

'We should go to the Isle of Wight.'

Wendy coughed on her cigarette. 'Please tell me you're kidding, David.'

'No, I'm serious. What's to stop us?'

'Well, nothing, really. But *Eastenders* is really good at the moment, and your lazy brother said he will finally come and fix the garage door this weekend. Plus, a holiday actually needs money.'

'Wendy, it's not a holiday. Trust me. We can afford the petrol.'

'Darling, we'll discuss it with the boys when they get home from college.'

'Right, well, today I will check the Camper van. Get the old girl ready for an adventure.'

She took a long drag on her cigarette. 'Yes, you do that, darling.'


Daniel and Rageh were just around the corner from the Webbs. They had played *Dead Rising 3* all night, interspersed with discussions about the end of the world. Rageh wanted to set off for the Isle of Wight immediately, and Daniel humoured him, just to keep the peace. By 4 a.m. they were talking about which relatives to invite along; most were discounted as being too boring to believe the threat, or too inconsequential to bother saving. They kept coming back to Daniel's cousin, Victoria, and Rageh's older sister, Deka. Victoria was fun and free-spirited, a self-employed nail technician, from nearby Braintree, who would come along at a moment's notice. Daniel fancied her quite a bit. Deka and her family deserved to live, but they were currently at *Disneyland*, Paris.

Rageh began to prepare food in Daniel's kitchen.

'No breakfast for me,' called Daniel, 'I'm going to bed.'

'I'm not making breakfast. I'm doing food to take with us.'

Daniel stepped into the small kitchen, frowning deeply. 'You're serious?'

Rageh looked at him. 'Deadly serious.'

'Must I believe you?'

'Why not? We have no jobs, we might as well go. It'll be fun. If I'm wrong, we come back. If I'm right...'

'There's tin foil in that cupboard.'

Rageh looked puzzled. 'Tin foil, to put on our heads, to shield our brains?'

'No, to put the sandwiches in. I'll go ring my cousin, Victoria.'

David Webb spent the morning checking the oil and water, and various other things, on his beloved VW Camper van. It was not customised in any way, and the pale blue bodywork had some rust spots, but he adored it - that, and his stock car, which he fine-tuned weekly before competitions. His neighbours just endured the hours of engine-revving, but he gave them no thought, whatsoever.

Wendy walked to the local branch of the *Halifax* bank, to make sure she had a lot of cash on her. She knew the boys would want to go, so there was nothing to discuss, really. Then she made lunch for her husband and herself, where they discussed the worst case scenario, (being murdered, which wasn't very nice with a tuna sandwich) and the route that they would take. It was not as if she had a job to go to; they could have a drive out to Southampton, the world would not come to an end, and they could come home again in time for the *Eastenders* omnibus episode on Sunday afternoon. For that reason, she brushed aside his worries about extended family members and friends. She wasn't going to drag her elderly parents along, her brother was a total idiot, and she wasn't going to make a fool of herself with her friends.

So, they were ready when the boys got home from college. There happened to be another Kamikaze attack on the news, that time in Oxford Street, Central London, so that gave David a way into opening the big talk. Kirk and Steven looked at each other over their crisps and *Mars* bar, respectively. They were an obnoxious pair, with similar scraggly face hair and random tattoos (Kirk had once lost a bet, which required him to get an Arsenal tattoo on his chest, which was now covered over by a dragon monstrosity). Both of the boys had girlfriends, charmless girls that actually meant very little to them, and missing college for a few days seemed a good plan. If they actually thought about it, perhaps their father's paranoia had something to it, and, being West Ham United fans, the

Wembley tornado had scared the life out of them. But, overall, they weren't bothered, and would just go along for the ride.

Victoria, Daniel's cousin, over in Braintree, was free and keen to go along with them. So, on an unseasonably wet and cold Summer's morning, Daniel and Rageh set out in Daniel's twelve-year-old Vauxhall Astra. They got the music banging on the radio, pulled off the estate and Daniel drove them away, straight into the side of a blue VW Camper van, which was turning into the road.

Rageh looked at Daniel. Daniel looked at Rageh.

'Was that my fault?' asked Daniel.

Rageh wasn't sure. But it was only a minor prang. Daniel tried to slowly reverse, but found that his bumper was connected to the bodywork of the van, and the big, greasy-looking driver was now out and waving frantically for him to stop. Daniel and Rageh got out of the Astra, only to have Wendy Webb in their faces.

'What's wrong with you, you donut!? Driving like an arse. Look what you've done.'

'You pulled out on me, woman,' argued Daniel.

'Who are you calling woman? What are you two, illegal immigrants, or something? I bet that shed's not even insured.'

Daniel and Rageh looked at each other, wondering about the use of the word, shed. They realised that it must be an insulting term for their vehicle.

David Webb had not even seen the Astra coming, and thought it his mistake, anyway. And, besides, the damage was trivial. The Camper van might be his most treasured possession, but it paled into insignificance compared to reaching the Isle of Wight. He tried to calm Wendy down. 'It's all right, Wendy. It's not worth worrying about. We have bigger fish to fry today.'

Wendy was dressed in jeans and a low, v-neck sweater, with a lot of cleavage on show. She decided to listen to her husband. Her two boys were there, and she didn't want them getting into any more trouble for battering those two idiots. She spotted that Rageh seemed to be fascinated with her bosom. She raised her hands and jiggled her breasts at him. Rageh was startled.

By chance, a police patrol car had been passing, and the two officers came over to take an interest in the accident. They walked with that slow amble that only policemen can master, one with hands on his utility belt and the other with thumbs inside his stab-proof vest.

David wanted to be on his way. 'It's nothing, officers. I don't want to make anything of it.'

PC Jagielka, the older of the two policemen, seemed happy to accept that. His colleague, PC Singh, equally so, although they were looking suspiciously at Daniel and Rageh. PC Singh bent to examine the damage, and at the same time checked Daniel's front left wheel.

'Oh, dear,' said PC Singh, standing. 'Oh, deary me.'

'Is something wrong?' asked PC Jagielka, with mock surprise.

'Without even testing the tread, I can tell that this tyre is illegal.'

'Is it, really? Shall we look at the others?'

Daniel pulled a face. Sarcastic police, all he needed.

'Is this your vehicle, sir?' PC Singh asked of Daniel. Daniel nodded. The other tyres produced similar pantomime performances from the policemen.

'Have you got your licence with you, sir?' asked PC Jagielka.

'Somewhere in the car.'

'Would you be so kind as to dig it out? Then we'll have a little chat in our vehicle.'

David stepped towards PC Jagielka. 'Officer, can we get going?'

'In a rush, are we, sir?'

'Er, not really.'

'Anyone about to have a baby?'

'No.'

'Well, please be patient. We'll be asking to see your documents, as well.'

Daniel went with the two policemen to their vehicle.

Rageh scratched his head and sighed, knowing that the car would be seized and removed. His blood started to boil with the fear of being too late.

'Chill out,' said David, noticing the man's agitation. 'You won't get nicked. Unless you *are* an illegal immigrant.'

'No, I'm not an illegal immigrant. We just don't need this. We have to be somewhere.'

'I know the feeling. Where are you off to?'

Rageh saw no reason not to tell this stranger where they were headed. 'The Isle of Wight.'

David was staggered. 'You're not!? That's where we're going.'

Rageh was as startled as when Wendy had jiggled her breasts at him. 'Honest?'

'We are, yeah.'

'So you see what's happening, too?'

'We do, yes. Well, I do. My wife is a bit of a septic.'

'You mean scéptic?'

'Oh, yeah. Whatever. Well, what a coincidence.'

Daniel returned from the police car, his face expressing deep unhappiness. 'They're taking the car. I'm getting a summons to court. Sorry, Rageh, mate.'

'Hey, cheer up,' said David. 'Plenty of room, come with us. I'll go tell the missus.'

'Really?' asked Rageh, astonished.

David walked off to find Wendy.

'Come with them where?' asked Daniel.

'They're going the same place as us.'

'They are?'

'I know, go figure!'

From behind the Camper van came the voice of Wendy Webb, 'You did *what*!?'

# 15

Bodie, Lily, Anthony, Dan and Professor Siddiq all sat on a low wall, outside a Ford car dealership in a suburb of Lincoln. They were eating a breakfast of crisps and drinking tea from polystyrene cups. The sun had yet to break through the morning overcast. They watched early commuters pass by, and a milkman in his float.

Lily was snuggled into Bodie's chest, feeling the cold.

'Just like being in Surabaya, isn't it?' he kidded.

'No, it's horrible. Bodie, last winter here I almost died. One day it got to -2. I couldn't believe it.'

Bodie laughed. 'Wait until you get me to Indonesia. I will suffer in the heat.'

She held him tighter. 'Promise me you'll come. You'll love it so much. Your bedroom will have air-conditioning.'

'My bedroom? Not our bedroom?'

Lily blushed. 'No, not our bedroom. Not until you marry me, and become a Muslim.'

'Become a Muslim?'

'Yes, it's very easy to do.'

Bodie realised that he had not actually considered that scenario before. He was cool with it. Lily was drinking her tea and grinning as she watched a mother walking her three little children to school, so he allowed the topic to drop.

Dan picked at his teeth, then said, 'So, what if we warn family members to stay indoors?'

'Futile, I would suggest,' answered Professor Siddiq.

That made everyone hunker down into their jackets, even more.

'We have no time to go north?' asked Anthony.

Nobody bothered to offer the obvious answer.

'My only family in England are in Newbury,' said Lily. 'On the way to Southampton.'

Professor Siddiq turned to her and smiled. 'Well, then, my dear Lily, we shall go via there.'

'Errrm,' said Anthony. 'We're not talking Granny in a wheelchair, are we? Sorry to be harsh.'

'No, just my brother and his wife.'

Dan laughed. 'Harsh. Harsh but fair.'

Then Dan went very quiet. Bodie lightly punched him on the thigh, sensing how his friend had started thinking of family to be left behind.

A car arrived at the showroom, from which a smartly

dressed woman emerged and walked to the showroom door, to be admitted by a security guard.

'We have life,' said Anthony.

They all discarded their breakfasts and walked to the showroom, where Bodie knocked on the glass door.

The Saleswoman came over, but didn't open the door. 'Sorry, we're not open yet.'

Bodie took out his gun and aimed it straight at her. The saleswoman fled.

'She's run off!' said Bodie.

'Shoot the door!' shouted Dan. 'Quick!'

Bodie fired one shot, low into the glass and it all shattered. They all entered, one by one, with Bodie and Dan running to apprehend the hysterical woman before she can use the phone on her desk.

'Don't be frightened,' said Bodie. 'We're not going to harm you. Just calm down.'

With the woman relatively under control, even though she was shaking and her hair was all over her face, Dan went in search of the security guard. He quickly returned with the man under gunpoint.

'We want the keys to a People Carrier,' said Bodie. 'That's all. Okay? Take us to the key cabinet.'

The saleswoman led the group upstairs to an office. She managed to control her shaking hands enough to open the door, then unlocked a big box on the wall, which contained hundreds of labelled keys.

'What model would you like?' asked the saleswoman.

Bodie and Dan laughed.

'That Galaxy, there,' pointed Bodie. 'That will do.'

Bodie took the car key. Dan frisked the guard and the saleswoman, taking their keys and cell phones. Then Dan ripped out the phones on the desks and threw them over the railing, onto the showroom floor. The guard and saleswoman were then locked in the office.

'We're sorry,' called Lily, as the group jogged downstairs.

It took a couple of minutes of frantic searching of the forecourt to find the Ford Galaxy, making Dan laugh at their criminal ineptitude, but then Anthony shouted, 'This one!' and they all piled in, with Bodie driving them away. They stopped shortly afterwards, on a street lined with cars, for Bodie to do his number plate swapping routine, one more time.

'I'm becoming an expert at this,' he told Lily, beside him. Lily caressed his head.

'I'll drive the first shift,' volunteered Dan.

Anthony was consulting a road atlas. 'I suggest we head towards Nottingham, and hit the M1 south from there.'

'Roger that,' said Dan, hopping into the driving seat, before starting to sing, '"Robin Hood, Robin Hood, riding through the glen..."'

'Victoria, looking hot, girl.'

Much to Wendy's chagrin, the Webbs and their two passengers had detoured to Braintree to pick up Daniel's cousin, Victoria. Daniel leant out of the window of the Camper Van to greet the girl, who stood in her short leather jacket, ripped light blue jeans and high-heeled boots, with a small bag at her feet.

Victoria looked with obvious disdain at the rusty old VW; at the slobs in the front seats (especially at the clearly hostile Wendy), at the two slavering teenage goons in the back, then at her cousin and his friend, who she vaguely recognised. 'Right, then,' she said, 'I'll give this a miss, thank you very much.' With that, she picked up her bag, spun on her heels and walked away.

'Victoria!?' called a perplexed Daniel.

But Victoria just kept on going.

'Well!' exclaimed Wendy. 'What a complete waste of time that was.'

At their six-bedroom home in a posh area of Milton Keynes, Vivienne Rhodes was worried about her husband, Brian; he had been very withdrawn since surviving the Wembley tornado disaster. He had taken time off work from his GP surgery, and tried to throw himself into his hobbies of gardening and woodwork, but he wasn't sleeping, and was constantly reliving the incident. He was considering paying a visit to his own doctor.

Vivienne carried a cup of tea out to her husband's work shed, down by the little stream that crossed their property. He paused from the garden table that he was crafting and accepted the cup.

'Thank you, darling,' he said. 'I thought you'd gone to your *Zumba* class.'

'I decided not to bother.' She passed her eyes over the table. 'How are you feeling?'

'Oh, I'm fine. You shouldn't pass up on your exercise for

me.' He indicated the table. 'What do you think?'

'It's as wonderful as all your creations, Brian. Darling, why don't we go away?'

'Abroad?'

She thought of the terrorist attacks at their two favourite destinations: Sharm El Sheikh and Kenya. 'No, staying in the UK. I thought, maybe, the Isle of Wight. We own our cottage there, we should use it more often.'

Brian thought about the whitewashed little property they had down there, and smiled. He put down his tea and hugged Vivienne. His pretty wife had a very sexy body, from all the exercise and, perhaps, not yet having children. They had been together since their university days, and had known no-one else. 'Yes, dear, that sounds like a wonderful idea. This weekend?'

'Why wait? Let's go today.'

'Today? I've got to finish... Oh, I suppose it can wait.' He smiled. 'Why not? I'll check the tyres on the Merc, and we can go after rush hour. How does that sound?'

'It sounds marvellous.'

They kissed, and she let him tidy up at his workshed. She returned to the house. She rang her parents, and her sister, letting them know they were going away for a few days. Then she went upstairs to pack. They would have a lovely, refreshing time on the Isle of Wight, and come back ready to face the world again.

For their evening meal they ordered in pizza. While Vivienne locked all the rooms and made sure nothing was left on, Brian loaded the cases into their Mercedes estate car. Then he wheeled the recycle bins down their long drive and left them out for the morning collection. It was a lovely, early evening, without a cloud in the sky. Since Wembley, he had been monitoring the weather forecasts, frightened that it would happen again, but he knew he had to pull himself together. Vivienne was amazing, and he owed her that, at least. She was locking the front door. He waited, then kissed her.

'Oh, frisky,' she said, smiling.

'I love you, Penguin.'

She giggled at his nickname for her. 'I love you, too.'

They got into the Mercedes and drove away, pausing when they saw dog-walking neighbours to tell them they were away for a while, then they all waved and Brian gunned the car down the road.

At a service station on the M1 motorway, Bodie and Lily sat at a wooden seat, with an umbrella above them, eating cheeseburgers. It was very busy, with lots of families around. They watched Anthony park up the Galaxy and walk over to them.

'That's full of fuel now,' said Anthony. 'It's expensive, this end of the world gig.'

Anthony pulled a face at them, Lily smiled back, and he went towards the building.

'Where are the others?' called back Anthony.

'On the games machines,' replied Bodie. 'Last play, and all.'

Anthony waved and disappeared inside.

'Anthony's a lovely man,' said Lily.

'He is, I agree.'

Lily put her legs over Bodie as they continued to watch the world go by. It was quite noisy with all the playing children. Suddenly, Lily burst into tears. Bodie pulled her close.

'Baby, what's wrong?' asked Bodie.

'Look at all the little children, Bodie. Look at the innocent little things. It's monstrous. Bloody monstrous.'

There was nothing Bodie could say to that.

Lily sniffled against his chest. 'Bodie, can you imagine it? You know, afterwards? If we survive, coming out to nobody being alive.'

'Well, you know me, babe. I'm not the sharpest tool in the box, but, yes, I have thought about it.'

'Will we be together still? I mean, I adore you, and everything, but we've only been dating a couple of months. We don't even live together properly.'

'Wow. You're a tough bird.'

'Sorry. But we're not exactly the love of each other's lives, are we?'

Bodie giggled. 'Behave, or I'll take you back to Old Leake.'

Lily laughed. 'Oh, I'm wetting your shirt.'

'Don't worry about it. Lily, baby, seeing as you have brought the topic up... I adore you, too...'

'Go on.'

'I don't want this to come out sounding bad.'

'Spit it out. It's all right.'

'Since the Professor came up with his theory, I've been thinking non-stop about, well, about the actual love of my life. She's called Maria. She lives in London. We dated for two years, before I met you, but her education got in the way. Plus, when my parents died, I wasn't very good company. I really want to save her.'

Lily sat up. Perhaps the extraordinary circumstances that they were living through kept her calm. She understood completely. 'You really gave that to me straight, didn't you? Well, I do actually understand what you are saying to me. I think we should try to save her. Yes, we should. Absolutely.'

'Thank you, Lily. You're an angel. You're amazing.'

Anthony, Dan and Professor Siddiq all came out to them, eating various chocolate bars and popcorn.

'What are you two talking about?' asked Dan.

'Bodie just decided to go and save the love of his life.'

Dan paused over his *Snickers* bar, confused. 'Eh? He what?'

# 16

Bodie was driving the Galaxy, with Anthony beside him in the passenger seat.

'The President and his family have left for their annual holiday,' said Anthony. 'I saw it on a TV screen back in the service station. No doubt, they're going to their safe place. Maybe they've created an eco-bubble at Camp David.'

Bodie giggled. 'Camp David. You know, if I'd been out when Dean arrived, we would have been oblivious to all this.'

They watched the road.

'Oh, and Man United lost again.'

Bodie smirked at that news.

'I wonder if we've got squatters in the apartment right now?' asked Anthony. 'After you left the place wide open.'

'I'm sorry about that. They'll be drinking your cheep beer.'

'Ah, good luck to them.'

Flashing blue lights took Bodie's attention in the rear view mirror. 'Dibble!'

Professor Siddiq sat up. 'I beg your pardon?'

'Police, Professor,' said Dan, 'Probably stopping all Ford Galaxies.'

'What do we do?' asked Professor Siddiq. 'We can't be arrested. We just can't. That will have us taken back to Lincoln, and remanded in custody. What could be worse?'

Bodie stopped the Galaxy on the hard shoulder of the motorway, with the police car stopping behind.

Bodie looked at Dan, 'We shoot them, as a last resort? They're going to die, anyway.'

Lily put a hand to her mouth, mortified. 'Oh, my God.'

'Yes, shoot them, I agree,' said Dan. 'As a last resort. But let's take their walkie-talkies and their car, just to give us more time.'

'Please be careful,' begged Lily.

Bodie and Dan got out of the Galaxy and looked back at the two policemen. Probably because they were faced with two men, both policemen exited their vehicle and approached. Bodie and Dan drew their guns in unison. The policemen panicked; one squatted down, while the other reached for his Taser.

'Stay still!' screamed Bodie. 'Stay still! Get on your faces! Get down on your faces and we won't kill you.'

Dan gesticulated with his gun. 'Down! Down!'

The policemen unwillingly complied, and Bodie and Dan

ran to them. Cars were flying by at great speed, causing a wash of air turbulence. Bodie kept the policemen covered, while Dan frisked them for their car keys, radios and Tasers.

'Up! Up! Shouted Bodie. 'Listen to me. You two cops get up that grass bank and go over the top. Get going! We won't shoot if you get out of sight.'

The policemen climbed the barrier and stumbled up the grassy bank.

'Out of sight!' shouted Bodie.

Once the heads of the policemen had vanished over the crest of the bank, Bodie took the keys to the patrol car. Dan ran back to the Galaxy with the equipment. The Galaxy drove off, followed by Bodie in the police car.

After about a mile, the Galaxy slowed onto the hard shoulder. Bodie took the police car up onto a small police lay-by, parked it, threw away the keys and ran to rejoin the others.

Back in the moving Galaxy, with Anthony driving, Bodie was embraced by Lily; they might be going to save another girl, but she still cared greatly for him.

Dan was examining his new toys: the Tasers. He started laughing.

The journey south continued. Lily had moved up front to chat to Anthony. She was hearing stories about Bodie's childhood, and giggling over it.

'What's that?' asked Bodie, from the very rear seats.

Lily smiled. 'Hearing about the time you did a martial arts kick at a table lying on its side, and how it spun round and knocked you over.'

'Oh, right. Anthony, tell her about the time you nearly killed me.'

Lily looked with anticipation at Anthony.

Anthony feigned to be struggling to remember. 'I was on my bike, Bodie was running. My front wheel hit the back of his legs, sending him flying forward. He landed with a bus stop pole between his legs, just as a bus flew by.'

Lily gasped, then giggled some more.

Professor Siddiq was fast asleep. Dan was slouched over two seats, looking back to Bodie, behind him.

Anthony looked over his shoulder. 'Does anyone think it's a good time to get off the motorway now? The alarm must have been raised, we'll have every policeman in the country looking for us.'

'Yes,' called Bodie. 'Get off at the next exit. We'll use the A-roads now.'

Dan sat up, wanting to chat with Bodie. 'Go on, then,' he whispered. 'Explain yourself. I remember how you were, with Maria. It was a bit volatile, but it was clearly love. Tell me what you're thinking.'

'I never stopped loving her. Okay, we split up, moved on, but the love is still in me. I can't just let her be murdered. Okay?'

'Yeah, okay.' Dan watched as they came off the motorway onto a normal road. 'Is it okay if I have a go at Lily, then?'

The two friends laughed madly, waking the Professor and causing Lily to look back at them with a frown.

The Webb group stopped at a service station on the M25.

Daniel and Rageh jumped out of the van to stretch their legs, both a little bit surprised to have stopped so soon, but then they saw the Webb clan stampede towards the fast food outlet. Daniel shrugged, then led Rageh into the complex, in search of sandwiches and coffee.

They inadvertently met up with the Webb boys later, and observed them shamelessly shoplifting from the newsagent shop. Outside, Steven and Kirk consumed their contraband sweets, giving some to their greedy parents.

Daniel whispered to Rageh, 'English pigs. You want to be saved, with these people?'

'All aboard!' called Wendy, who seemed to have perked up after her fast food meal.

Daniel was last in, sliding the door shut. They moved as far as the petrol station. David got out to fill the tank.

'Are we all right, boys?' asked Wendy, turning back in her seat.

'Yes, thank you,' answered Daniel.

'We'll soon be there. Find out if we are to live or die.' She fanned her face. 'Ooh, it's getting warm. Come on, David, hurry up, let's get some air flowing through the vents.'

David Webb climbed back into the driver's seat and headed them back out onto the motorway.

Daniel looked at Rageh. 'Did he not pay for the fuel?'

Rageh just grinned, sheepishly.

David slowly got the Camper van up to speed, in the inside lane. So far, he had suffered Radio 1, but it was time for his Classic FM. As he was changing the channel, his wife screamed.

'What!? What!?' cried David, grabbing the wheel with both hands. 'I was only changing the channel, for heaven's sake.'

Everyone in the back had jumped out of their skins at Wendy's shriek. Wendy had seen a man jump from a bridge, several cars ahead. David had to slow, with all the traffic ahead showing red brake lights.

'It was one of those Kamikaze terrorists,' said Wendy. 'I saw him jump.'

David put on the handbrake and looked at his distraught wife.

'Hug her, then,' said Kirk, in a deadpan voice.

Daniel looked at Rageh. It was the first time they had heard one of the boys speak. Rageh shrugged.

David hugged his wife. 'Are you sure, Wendy? It's not much of a terrorist act to just jump in front of moving cars.'

'Well, a suicide, then. I saw it. It was horrible.'

'There, there. It's all right.'

Rageh sighed back into his seat. A terrorist act or a simple suicide - they were not going anywhere soon.

Twenty minutes later, with the police and ambulance service on the scene, and with hundreds of people milling around beside their stationary vehicles, on both carriageways, the Webb group were starting to get annoyed. Daniel was fed up, but trying at least to get some sun on his face. Rageh and David were more distressed at the delay, as they saw the bigger picture, while Wendy and her sons were more naturally impatient - Wendy was known to complain at waits at Doctor's surgeries or long queues in a supermarket. She looked ahead towards the bridge, with all its flashing blue lights. That kind of thing had happened to her before on a motorway; not a jumper, but some disturbed teenage boy threatening to commit suicide. After ten minutes, which made her late for a hairdressing appointment, she had stormed to the front of the queue of traffic and shouted up at the "sad moron" to get on with it and jump.

'I'm going to see what's happening,' said Wendy.

'Will that do any good, darling?' asked David.

'I just want to see why they can't just drag the sorry mess to the side.'

'It's a crime scene, darling. They have to do things properly.'

Wendy pulled a face. 'Whatever.'

Wendy, Kirk and Steven walked through the mass of people. She pushed aside a small boy who was practising on his hoverboard, and pulled a face at a man whose radio was far too loud. Up at the front, they saw three ambulances and four police cars. Several vehicles had crashed, as they tried to avoid the falling man. There were people up on the bridge, and Wendy watched with interest as a scuffle seemed to break out. Several Police Community Support Officers, which Wendy held in total contempt, were struggling to stop three Asian men from climbing the parapet. Then the men were preparing to jump, offering up prayers, and Wendy realised with horror that the original jumper had just been a decoy to bring emergency personnel below the bridge. The three men dived off together. The image imprinted itself on Wendy's brain before she spun away, grabbing her sons, as the terrible thing took place.

# 17

Aaron Ford adjusted his back-to-front *Kansas City Royals* baseball cap, flicked sweat from his eyebrows, and again considered whether or not he was enjoying his vacation to England. Salisbury Cathedral had been spectacular, Stonehenge had proved rather disappointing and overcrowded, while all the London sights had been just as expected - he was working his way around the south coast; mainly doing farm work, fruit picking, with one bartender position in a Winchester pub. So far, all the English people he had met had been wonderful. Nobody had been anti-American, or xenophobic in any way. He was yet to go north, where the accent problem would start to be a problem, though.

Nineteen-year-old Aaron was the youngest of eight kids

from Platte Woods, just outside Kansas City, Missouri. He was a very good looking guy, well-built, but surprisingly quite shy, and not into the kinds of things that people would expect of him; he liked English literature, all types of architecture and had just started to get into drone technology. On arrival in England, six weeks earlier, he had bought a drone, flown it around Wimbledon Common (been told off by the police), and now it filled most of the rucksack which he carried around with him.

His current employment was on a farm near Ashford in Kent, where, from dusk 'til dawn, he and thirty or so other foreigners, picked strawberries. He actually detested strawberries, always had, so, unlike everyone else, he never secretly ate any. The sole reason for him not moving on was standing quite near to him, with hands on her sexily wide hips, her blonde, slightly dreadlocked, hair in a bandana, looking with an amused expression at his slacking.

'Hey!' she called. 'There is no break yet.'

Her name was Ana, from one of the Baltic states (he could never remember which one) and she was amazingly cute - it was that special cuteness that defies description, just a wonderful, all-over glow of youth and vivacity to her. Nothing romantic had happened between them, but she clearly fancied him, and had focussed on him in the local pub, to the detriment of guys from her own country. Aaron hoped he wasn't blushing.

'You're not my boss,' he joked.

'That's a good thing, no? I would have sacked your butt.'

'You would have smacked my butt?'

'Sacked your butt!'

'Well, if you sack me, and I leave, we won't have our beautiful relationship.'

It was Ana who blushed, instead. For a shy man, Aaron was delighted with his cheeky banter.

But then she turned away, back to work, in the football-sized polytunnel in which they slaved. He watched her for a moment. She blew his mind. But those strawberries...

Aaron got back to work. In due course, back home in the States, he wanted to become an architect, but his family knew he had to get some of his wanderlust out of his system. The previous year he had visited parts of France and Italy, and this trip had started first in Berlin, a place that fascinated him. Still to do on his English adventure, was to drift north and visit some of the literary places, especially the home of Thomas Hardy, and he might even have time to catch a train to Edinburgh and experience the streets walked by Ian Rankin's *Inspector Rebus*.

His mind started to wander to other jobs he could be doing, besides strawberry picking. Digging ditches would be better. Mucking out at a stables. Suddenly Ana was beside him. There was no definitive perfume, but she smelled great, completely taking his mind off horse manure.

'Are you coming to the pub tonight?' she asked.

'Well, Ana, that does seem to be the only option for socialising around these parts.'

'Maybe, you know, we can walk there together?'

Aaron beamed from ear to ear. 'That would be nice.'

It went very dark in the polytunnel - occasionally it got dim, if clouds obscured the sun, but it had gone really dark.

'We're having a storm,' said Aaron.

Ana's eyes became doleful. 'I don't like storms. I hope there's no lightning.'

He tried to cheer her by laughing, and then thought he should give her a comforting hug, but he had to abort the movement of his arm as her cell buzzed in her jeans pocket.

Aaron looked the full length of the polytunnel; he had never seen it that dark before, they would have to stop working until the storm passed. Then he saw colleagues jumping around, at the far end. More horseplay wouldn't go down well with the farmer. Their shouts reached him. Something seemed wrong. Perhaps the rain was coming into the tunnel. Someone had said something about a tornado in London. He kept watching, until the storm seemed to engulf the workers and he couldn't see them anymore. He made Ana turn to look, also.

'What's happening?' she asked.

She dropped her cell, as a wall of blackness rushed towards them.

'Run!' screamed Aaron, pushing her in the side.

Before they could react, as in a car crash, a wave of filthy, all-encompassing darkness filled their worlds. Ana screamed. Aaron tried to cover her up. From the feeling, the sheer creepy-crawliness of it, he knew that it was flies. Millions, billions of flies. They were in his ears, up his nose; Ana was screaming through her fingers. The sensation was simply appalling, almost like drowning in insects. It was disgusting, terrifying, and, more worryingly, stopping them from breathing.

Aaron's brain tried to compute what was happening - a plague of flies had descended on the farm. The noise was maddening. From somewhere deep inside, he found the strength to not give in to it. In fact, he whipped Ana up in his arms and hustled them down the tunnel. His lungs ached, the sensation on his skin made him want to fall to the ground and dig into the soil, but he pushed on, finally making it to an exit. Once outside, the plague still surrounded them, but at least they could breathe. Aaron took in great gulps of air, plus a few dozen flies, and then he managed to squint his eyes as he made his way to a farm Land Rover. The vehicles were never locked. Still holding the cowering, shaking Ana, he opened the passenger door and deposited the girl inside. He skipped through the fog of flies and got in at the other side. Slamming the door was heaven. They were still bothered by some flies, which had entered the car with them, and were spitting out others, but they were free to recover. Ana, however, was still having a panic attack, struggling to breathe while she wafted wildly at the pests with one hand, wiping her face with the other. Aaron took her in his arms.

'Ana, close your eyes and hug the seat,' he told her. 'I'm going to kill the flies in here.'

Then he rolled up a magazine and set about the task.

# 18

Bodie's group arrived in Teddington, south west London, in the early evening. With Dan driving, they toured the area until Bodie got his bearings.

'Take a left, Dan,' directed Bodie. 'Keep slow. This looks like the place. I remember that park.'

Everyone was staring out at the big detached houses. They had to be a million pounds plus. All the cars on the drives were BMWs, Mercedes or 4x4s.

'It's a posh area,' said Lily, jealousy of Maria beginning to show its face.

'Here, here, stop here,' said Bodie.

They parked the Galaxy on the road; everyone got out and walked up the well-lit drive. Bodie started to think that perhaps he should have made them wait in the van, but by then Dan had rung the bell. They waited, but nobody answered.

'They might not even live here, any more,' suggested Lily.

Bodie was about to knock, when the hall light came on. Slowly the front door opened, revealing an old woman in a wheelchair.

Anthony half turned away. 'Oh, my mistake. The granny in the wheelchair is here, not at Lily's.'

'Hello? Yes?' asked the old lady.

'Mrs Cowfield?' asked Bodie. 'Maria's grandmother?'

Dan looked at Anthony, both miming the unusual "Cowfield" surname.

The old lady just kept looking at them.

'We're friends of Maria,' continued Bodie. 'Is she here?'

'She's at work,' said Mrs Cowfield. 'Would you like to come in and wait?'

'Oh, we wouldn't want to impose.'

'Nonsense, nonsense,' said Mrs Cowfield, backing herself up. 'I've not spoken to a soul all day. I'm about to have my supper, though. Come in. Come in.'

Everyone paraded into the house. They were settled into the lounge, and within ten minutes, with Lily's help, they all had a nice bowl of Minestrone soup on their laps, with fresh bread, watching *Strictly Come Dancing* on the TV. Anthony suddenly laughed at how surreal it all was.

'I'm sorry, Mrs Cowfield,' Bodie apologised for Anthony. 'My friend is a little tired.'

Mrs Cowfield did not seem to mind. She was quite happy to

have some guests there with her.

'I like a good quiz, you know,' said Mrs Cowfield. 'Shall we have a game of *Trivial Pursuit*?'

The men pulled their faces, but Lily was charmed by the old lady. 'Of course. We have to wait for Maria, anyway.'

'Mrs Cowfield?' asked Bodie, 'do you know where Maria works?'

'Oh, yes, dear.'

Bodie waited, but she didn't say anything more. He looked at Dan. 'We go and get her?'

Dan nodded.

'Mrs Cowfield,' continued Bodie. 'Do you know where Maria's parents are?'

'Oh, yes, dear.'

Lily leant towards Mrs Cowfield. 'Could you tell us where?'

'On the P&O cruise ship, Oriana, off the coast of Norway.'

'Oh,' said Lily, smiling.

Lily and Bodie removed and washed up the supper bowls. Back in the lounge, Mrs Cowfield directed Lily to where the board came was, in a cupboard.

'A quick game?' asked Lily, looking at Bodie and Anthony.

'A quick one,' said Anthony.

So, they gathered around the coffee table and played *Trivial Pursuit*. Lily's first question to Bodie was, 'What do Australians call Austria?'

'Eh?' asked Bodie.

'Oh, sorry. What do Austrians call Austria?'

They all laughed.

'Osterreich,' answered Bodie, impressing Lily.

Bodie rolled the dice and continued. Lily's next question was, 'Ian Gresham wrote the lyrics to *Porgy and...*?'

'Ian Gresham?' asked Bodie. She showed him the question card. 'Oh, Ira Gershwin. *Porgy and Bess*. Have you not played this before, Lily?'

'No, never.'

There was more hilarity. Bodie rolled the dice again.

Lily's third question to Bodie was, 'Who wrote the classic novel, *Worthington Heights*?'

Anthony was still blackly amused by the evening's events. He stood at the Cowfield's front door, waving Bodie and Dan off towards a waiting taxi. 'Okay, we'll stay here with Mrs Cowfield. The *X-Factor* is on now. What do you think about that? If you're not back by 3 a.m. we're leaving for Newbury.'

'We understand,' called back Bodie.

'Good luck!'

The taxi took Bodie and Dan into the West End. The area they were dropped at was swarming with young people having a good time.

'My first time in the West End of London,' said Dan. 'Look, there's a sign for Soho, but I'm such a good mate, I'll stay with you.'

'That's very good of you. The taxi driver said the restaurant we want is down that pedestrianised way, there.'

'Then let's go.'

They started to walk, before Dan indicated a Takeaway food shop.

'You're still hungry?' asked Bodie. 'After Granny Cowfield's soup?'

'I could just go a pizza right now.'

They stepped into the shop, waited their turn, then ordered a large pepperoni pizza, leaving with it in a cardboard box.

'After this,' said Dan, 'I'll have a few beers at the restaurant bar, while you tell the girl that her family are about to die.'

As Dan finished talking, the pizza box was snatched from his hand by a man leaning out of a passing car. The car turned a corner, with the man cheering as if he had scored a winning goal, and disappeared into the night.

Dan looked aghast at Bodie. 'Can you believe that just happened?'

Bodie could only smirk.

They walked on, coming across the correct restaurant: the one that Mrs Cowfield had told them about. They entered the darkened foyer.

'Well, I look smart enough,' pointed out Dan, 'but I don't know about you, Bodie.'

At the mention of the name Bodie, a female member of staff spun around quickly. She held menus in her arms and was about to seat a couple of diners. Bodie recognised his ex-girlfriend, Maria. She had jet black hair, just like Lily, but of course her face was much paler.

'Bodie! I don't believe it.'

'Yep, it's me.'

Maria gathered her wits and asked a colleague to sit the customers at their table. Then she threw herself into Bodie's embrace. 'What are you doing here?'

'Looking for you.'

'It's so great to see you. Wow.'

Maria's colleague quickly returned, keen to know who the two good-looking guys were, especially the cool, hippy one. Maria introduced Bodie to her.

'Bodie?' asked the girl. 'Like in the 80's cop show?'

Bodie scowled a little bit. 'No.'

Dan cut in, asking Maria, 'Do you have potato skins here?'

'No, we don't, sorry.'

Maria tugged Bodie away to the side, so they could talk privately.

'I'll be at the bar,' said Dan.

Maria took Bodie's hands in her own. 'Bodie, as I live and breathe.'

Their life together game flooding back, and feeling of love resurfaced.

'What time do you get off?' he asked her.

She laughed. 'I bet you've said that before. Errrm, soon. Can you wait half an hour?'

'Yeah, sure.'

'Okay. It really is lovely...'

A massive bang, outside in the street, brought shock and screaming inside the restaurant. Maria jumped against Bodie. There then came the pop, pop, pop of automatic gunfire, terrifying Maria, Bodie equally so, as he pulled her further into the restaurant, with customers and staff hurrying away. Bartenders were leaping their counter to get out.

Dan ran to join Bodie and Maria, as they moved towards the kitchen area. Bodie glanced back, seeing people running down the street, and then the unmistakable silhouette of a man with a gun held out in front of him, firing right there outside the restaurant. Bodie and the others could not get through the squash of people in time, so fell behind a till station. Maria was shaking with fear. Dan brought out his gun, which freaked Maria out even more. Bodie drew his weapon, with a shaky hand. The two men locked eyes, both thinking, *This is it! No further journey to the Isle of Wight. It ends here and now, in London.*

The terrorist entered the restaurant and shot several diners who had been too slow to flee. The echoing noise was dreadful, followed by a chilling silence. The terrorist moved further into the restaurant, shooting far left, failing to hit a waitress who managed to barge through a fire exit and escape, and then fired ahead towards the noise in the kitchen. He was no more than twenty feet from their hiding group.

Dan was trying to move, trying to pull free of Bodie's desperate hold on his clothing, and he popped up to his feet. He aimed and shot at the terrorist, hitting him in the upper left chest area, spinning the man. Instantly, the terrorist returned fire. Dan fired again, emptying his weapon, hitting the terrorist once more. The terrorist aimed at Dan and, very deliberately, shot him dead.

Despite Maria's desperate attempts to restrain him, Bodie threw himself from the cover of the till station and fired at the terrorist until his gun was empty; several shots hit the man's body armour, but one bullet went straight through his throat, killing him outright, making him drop backwards.

Time seemed to stop for Bodie, with just the sound of his heart beating madly. Then he regained control of his mind and scrambled over to Dan, distraught to see his friend lying lifeless on the cold floor. There was blood everywhere, but Dan appeared to be peacefully asleep. It was simply too much to take; Bodie's whole being ached with distress and horror. He had gotten Dan involved in the madness, in the first place, and now he had gotten him killed. Bodie was too shocked to cry, or even blink. He just sat there. Finally, he squeezed Dan's shoulder and averted his eyes. Maria was whimpering, so Bodie slid back to her, covered her mouth with his hand, and they both lay there shaking, for what seemed like an age.

Professor Siddiq was climbing the walls with impatience to get going. He was still in the Cowfield living room, unable to watch any more inane television programmes. Anthony was upstairs on the Cowfield's computer, catching up on world events. Lily was sitting with Mrs Cowfield, assisting her with her *Daily Mail* crossword. She kept glancing at the Professor.

'Salman?' she said, deliberately using his first name. 'Are you all right? You're worrying me.'

'I'm just keen to get going, Lily.'

'I know. So am I. Would you like another cup of tea?'

Professor Siddiq stood up. 'I'm swimming in the stuff. You know what, I think I want to look at the River Thames, for the first time in my life. I believe it's only a few streets away from here.'

'Oh? Are you sure that's wise?'

'It should only take half an hour or so. I doubt they'll be back much before midnight.'

'Shall I come with you?'

'I'd be delighted if you would. I'll go and tell Anthony. You tell Mrs Cowfield that we're just popping out.'

Professor Siddiq went upstairs, used the bathroom, then looked in on Anthony, in the study. 'Any news, Anthony?'

'Nothing earth shattering. I've just emailed family members, and my girl in Sheffield.'

'Oh, I didn't know. I'm sorry. By the way, Lily and I are going out for a breath of fresh air.'

Anthony thought about objecting, but then nodded. 'Please be careful, Professor.'

Lily met him in the hall, and they walked out to the street.

'Right,' said Professor Siddiq, getting his bearings. 'We'll go that way.'

They walked, talking intermittently. Lily felt like holding his hand, but decided against it. Crossing a road, Lily stumbled in a pothole. Professor Siddiq steadied her.

'So many potholes,' said Lily, 'For a First World country.'

Professor Siddiq giggled, making Lily do the same.

'What?' she asked.

'Oh, I've just got a theory about potholes. The government gives so many millions of pounds in foreign aid, yet there's not a smooth road in the country. Yes, I know, it's to relieve poverty. But, I just think the pothole situation is deliberate. It's like owners of football teams; they want to give the fans lots of one-nil wins, with a few draws, and the occasional defeat, because if your team keeps winning three and four-nil, you expect it all the time. The government winds up the population on things like potholes to keep them expecting a draw, or a narrow win. It keeps order.' He giggled again.

'Anyway, that's my idea.'

'I like your idea, Salman.'

'Thank you. Now, tell me about your brother.'

'My brother? His name is Ari. He's so clever. He does something in the pharmaceutical industry. His English wife, Sarah, is a local MP.'

'Is she really? What party?'

'She's an Independent, I think.' Lily's head dropped. 'I don't suppose it matters any more.'

Professor Siddiq chose to hold Lily's hand. 'There, there. Don't give up hope. We shall get to the sacred isle and find sanctuary. Can you smell the river yet?'

She laughed. 'I don't think it smells these days. Professor... sorry, Salman... what if we don't make it? What if we are caught outside? And die? I'm only eighteen years old.'

That made him sigh deeply. He wondered whether to change the subject. 'Lily, I don't know if this is at all relevant, but there is an idea, floating around...' She urged him to go on. 'When a child dies, and it devastates the family... what if, in another dimension, the child doesn't die, but grows up? Because, what is the point of it all? How can something so amazing as a child die, and not have a life? It may die again at fifteen. But, then, in another dimension, it grows up to have its own family, and to watch its parents pass away. Or, a man is killed on his motorbike, again devastating his family? A little girl grows up without a father. But, in that other dimension, the father survives the crash and is there to give his daughter away at her wedding.'

They were approaching the slow-moving river. Lily took in

everything Professor Siddiq was saying, but it was heavy stuff for her.

'Sorry,' he said. 'I was just bumbling into the idea of life continuing, whatever happens. You go on to marry your Bodie and have four kids.'

Lily snorted. 'You're forgetting why we're in London, Salman.'

'Yes, of course. Well, you'll meet another good man. Anyway, enough of that, we're going to be fine. While the general population sits blindly in ignorance, we are pushing on, and will find a way in.'

The two of them hugged. In doing so, they were unaware of a group of four white youths approaching them. It was a shock to find themselves surrounded.

'What have we got 'ere, then?' asked one of the youths. 'Two of those Kamikazes. What are you two doing 'ere? Plotting something?'

Lily was instantly frightened, more so for Professor Siddiq. She felt him tense before he released her. Then she was expecting, with him being a distinguished academic, to attempt some form of communication, even with scum of the earth. But, instead, Professor Siddiq launched a tremendous head butt on the youth who had spoken to him. That left only three, and they instantly laid into the Professor with fists and kicks. Lily screamed and tried her best to defend the Professor.

The brawl left the pavement and carried on across the riverbank. Professor Siddiq was fighting back, as best he could.

'Get away, Lily!' he shouted.

'I'll go for Anthony!' screamed Lily.

As she tried to get back to the road, one of the youths grabbed her by the front of her shirt. Lily bit his hand so fiercely that blood spurted up as she broke free. She started running, but stopped as she heard more voices, and had the beam of a torch flood over her.

'Stay there, young lady!'

It was the police: a male and a female. Lily ignored the command and continued to edge away. The two police officers hurried to the fight. The female officer used her pepper spray and the male had his baton out, striking out at knees. Two of the youths squirmed free, but one was detained by the male officer. Professor Siddiq, bloodied and weak, could only kneel there in the mud while the female officer handcuffed him.

Totally distraught, Lily fled back to the Cowfield residence.

# 19

Aaron Ford detested strawberries even more now; he never wanted to see another one for the rest of his life.

Two female workers, both students from the Czech Republic, had tragically died during the bizarre fly infestation event. One other girl, who suffered from asthma, was currently in hospital. The police had taken statements from Aaron and Ana. The farm was currently inundated with Department of Health and other Governmental officials, conducting an investigation.

Ana was determined to leave, and go home. Aaron, who had comforted her all through the day, and who was beginning to develop stronger and stronger feelings for the girl, could hardly try to dissuade her, given what had happened. So, they packed their things and caught the last bus to Ashford. From there, Ana could get the Eurostar train to Paris, and then work her way north from there.

They were the only passengers on the bus, and sat on the back like school kids. At the station, she insisted that he must not wait around with her. That hit him like a punch to the stomach, bringing back all his shyness. Realising her mistake, Ana took his face in her rough hands (three hard months of strawberry picking) and looked him in the eye.

'Thank you for saving my life, Mr Aaron Ford. You are a very special man. I will find you in the future. Now, go, get on with your English experience. I shall find you again, I promise.'

Then she kissed him. She picked up her bags and walked into the train station terminal, without looking back.

'You stay safe,' he called.

Aaron watched her, until she was out of sight. Feeling very lost, he adjusted his *Royals* cap, picked up his belongings and turned away. He could see a coffee shop, not too far away, so he went in there and bought his favourite drink. Sitting himself down near the window, he pondered his next move. He had never encountered the death of anyone before, not even his grandparents. The terrible event on the farm made him want to get on the next flight home. But then he bucked up his ideas, still felt good being in England. He would call his folks, reassure them of his wellbeing, and then he would move on to the next stage of his travels. But where? He took out a small map which he always carried in his rucksack. He also had a little black book with connections and possible places to seek employment. His eyes settled on the name and address of his English *GoodReads* friend, which was a website for book lovers, with the note that he should look him up, if ever he was in England. That seemed a good plan. He took out his cell and dialled the number in Newbury, Berkshire.

The cruise ship which had been damaged by the terrorist rockets in the Suez Canal had turned back to Southampton. The dead and injured, along with 95% of the passengers, had been disembarked at Port Said and flown home to the UK. Margaret and Barry Fallon were among the 5% who flat-out refused to fly, under any circumstances, and so were staying with the ship, as it limped home for repairs. Their friends, Janet and Frank, had decided to fly home.

It was a surreal experience, to say the least: a ghost ship, Barry described it as. He and his wife were upgraded to a suite with a balcony, but only because their cabin had been destroyed in the attack, along with all their clothes. The staff remained upbeat and attentive. There were no longer any buffets set out on deck, but the couple ate all their meals in one of the four restaurants. Strangely, the passengers staying on didn't gather together (there was no Dunkirk spirit), everyone remained as before, so there were great swathes of empty tables between diners.

Barry could just about see the damage on the port side, if he leant over the railing. In truth, he was enjoying the trip more. He could swim in the pool without hindrance, take Margaret to the cinema without anybody else being there. Remarkably, the show went on in the theatre; full performances, sometimes to only six or seven people. Their suite was absolutely amazing, with champagne being brought by their steward every day. Plus, Barry knew that it would all be free, and with a free cruise and compensation awaiting them in the future.

They had been in contact with their children via *Skype*, who would be waiting for them in Southampton. And so, they moved at a slow pace across the Mediterranean. The weather was superb, too. They stopped at Malta, to take on board extra engineers, who had flown in from the UK. Barry wanted to enquire whether they could go ashore for the day, but Margaret stopped him from making a fool of himself.

That evening it was formal dining in the restaurant. Barry looked oddly at his wife when she brought his tuxedo out of the wardrobe, but they both got dressed up and, along with the only other two couples there that evening, they sat at the Captain's table.

After a couple of days, they passed through the Straits of Gibraltar, out into the Atlantic. That was where TV News helicopters came over to film them. Once out into the fairly choppy Bay of Biscay, smaller vessels came along as support. The ship started to struggle, and finally it was decided that she should be stopped for a while off the coast of France, so that water could be pumped out of the lower decks. There was no danger of her sinking; it was just making it an even longer crawl back to Southampton.

Barry played shuffleboard on the stationary ship with a fellow passenger who told him that his family was not waiting for him in port, but his lawyer certainly was.

Sarah Fransisca-Smith MP completed her weekly surgery with constituents at her offices, said goodnight to her assistant, Frances, and headed home in her white BMW 1 series. She loved that car. Ari, her husband, said it pulled to the left, but she never felt it do that.

First, she stopped at her dentist to make an appointment for a check-up, then she popped into Waitrose for a few things for her and her husband's dinner. On the way out, she checked her cute, bobbed-blonde appearance in a plate glass window, and was happy with what she saw.

Young for a Member of Parliament, Sarah was 27-years-old. She was the daughter of a popular, retired, Lib Dem MP, and had always been interested in politics. She was quite a celebrity in the Newbury area, constantly having strangers come up to her for a chat, or a rant about something that was wrong, in their opinion. It was coming up for the two years anniversary of marriage to her beloved Ari, who she had met while back-packing around Asia with friends on her gap year from Cambridge University. Her mother (and his) kept asking about children, but, for the moment, her career came first.

She loved Ari beyond life itself. He was adorable, and the perfect husband, always supporting her through the trials and tribulations of being an MP. As she drove home along twisty, country lanes, lost in the fun of the BMW, her mind drifted away to him. Perhaps children should become a priority? She could take maternity leave. He would make such an amazing father. That made her grin. She was very happy with her life.

At their five-bedroom, Mock Tudor house in Newbury, Ari

Fransisca loved his ride-on lawnmower - sometimes he considered offering to do his neighbours' lawns for free, just to prolong the fun. Off work for a few days, he did the front and back lawns, all the time keeping his cell phone on, in case Lily rang again. His kid sister had scared the pants off him the last time she had called. He had tried to demand that she tell him where she was, so he could go pick her up. But, after a lot of persuasion, he agreed to trust her judgment. But he had expected her to call again, and when he tried her number it just went straight to voicemail.

His wife, Sarah, had attempted to ease his worries, telling him what a smart cookie Lily was. His wife and sister got on very well, on the few times they had met. Sarah was a genuinely lovely human being, but also an only child, so perhaps that made her so close to Lily.

Ari decided to go outside again to wash his Audi A5 - one week outside its warranty, the water pump had gone, which was expensive, and he had the mechanic's oily fingerprints all over the bonnet. As he finished, out on their wide, sweeping gravel drive, he heard a vehicle coming down the lane. It was too early for Sarah to be getting home, so he took an interest in it. As it came into view, he recognised the car belonging to their Next courier who, due to Sarah's prolific shopping habits, was a regular visitor. Ari wandered down to the gate to accept the parcel and put an illegible scribble on the lady's handset.

'I'll see you tomorrow,' he joked, and the courier laughed and waved goodbye.

Ari decided to go into the kitchen and make his favourite Indonesian coffee. While waiting on the kettle to boil, he opened his laptop, to check whether Lily had contacted him that way - negative. Then he looked at *GoodReads*, his favourite book website. Oh, four new messages - he loved getting messages on *GoodReads*. He made his coffee and settled down on a stool, at the island. An Indonesian friend was just saying hello, and three American friends were recommending books to him that they had just reviewed. The last of the messages came from a woman called Lisa, in Dallas; now, while he was 100% committed to Sarah, and deliriously happy with her, it was a tiny bit exciting to be in communication with an attractive American lady.

He politely replied to everyone, then perused the book giveaways, entering a few, although he was yet to win anything. His coffee was perfect. Basically, his life in England was perfect. However, if he had met Lisa all those years ago, he might be an American citizen, by then.

The sound of Sarah's car crunching up their drive brought him round. He went out to greet her, and they hugged and kissed, and he took the shopping in for her.

'A cup of tea, darling?' he suggested.

Sarah kicked off her shoes and hugged him from behind. 'That would be lovely.'

'Did you have a good meeting?'

'Yes, very productive. I'll have my tea and then maybe let you scrub my back in the tub.'

Ari grinned. 'That sounds like a plan.'

Their evening progressed normally. After a frolic in the bath, and a good dinner, they settled down to watch *The People vs. OJ Simpson*, which had been saved on *Sky plus* for a while.

The phone in the hall disturbed them. Ari jumped up, hoping it was Lily. Sarah paused the programme and looked closely at his face when he returned, a few minutes later.

'Was it Lily?'

'No.'

He returned to her embrace on the sofa. He clearly had something to tell her, though his teasing suggested that it was not too serious. 'Darling, you know when couples sometimes meet other couples on holiday, and exchange details, saying that they should stop by if they are ever in the area?'

'Yes...'

'Well, errm, one of my *GoodReads* friends is in the country, and asked to pay a visit.'

'Really? Who?'

'An American, called Aaron.'

Sarah laughed. 'Oh, thank God. I thought you were going to say it was a woman.'

Ari laughed. 'A woman!? Haha! No, no, don't be silly. He's a nice guy. He comes from Kansas City. You don't mind, do you?'

'Of course not, darling. I'm actually intrigued. We don't have enough visitors here. When is he coming?'

'He said tomorrow.'

'Tomorrow? Well, I can't wait to meet your American book friend. I'm just sorry it wasn't Lily on the phone. I'm so worried about her.'

The telephone rang again.

'He's changed his mind,' joked Sarah. 'He's going

somewhere better.'

Ari jumped up. 'This will be Lily.'

Sarah waited, listening to try to hear her husband's excitement. But instead, he called her through, gave her the phone and left her alone.

After half a minute, Sarah came back to the lounge and snuggled up to Ari.

'What was that?' he asked.

'I'm not sure. It was a notification that we are to receive a hand-delivered document from the Metropolitan Police this evening. Every MP in the country is to get one.'

'How bizarre, baby.'

'I know. Very.'

It was ten o'clock when a marked police car led a black BMW up to the Fransisca house. Ari was just making coffee. He watched through the kitchen window as Sarah met the police officers, taking the senior ones into her study, and pointing the junior ones towards the kitchen.

So, Ari made coffee for the two constables, who stood, intimidating in their stab vests, boots and utility belts. They had tasers, Ari noticed, but no firearms.

'So, you're from the Met?' asked Ari, to make conversation.

Both policemen nodded. The trip was bizarre in the extreme, and they were happy for a hot drink.

'This is awesome, Mr Fransisca,' said PC Dooley, tasting the coffee.

Ari felt proud. 'The best Indonesian coffee.'

'Really good,' agreed PC Holt.

'I've got lots, you must take some.'

'Oh, we couldn't,' protested PC Dooley.

'But I insist.'

'Okay, then.'

Sarah was not long with the senior officers who had travelled up from Scotland Yard. She only had to prove her and her husband's identity, and then she signed for an official document from No. 10 Downing Street. The officers, as puzzled as she was, took their leave, and the two vehicles departed.

Sarah joined Ari in the kitchen and insisted on a massive hug. Ari kissed his wife's head. Sarah took a knife from the block and opened the manila envelope. She quickly scanned it. Ari watched his wife's preened eyebrows going up and down.

'Well..?' he asked.

'Darling, it appears we've been summoned, along with every MP and their families, to the Isle of Wight. That's where the government is at the moment. We are to be ready to be collected at seven o'clock, tomorrow morning. What on earth can it mean?'

Ari hugged Sarah. He was lost for words.

# **20**

Anthony opened the front door to admit both Bodie and the pretty brunette girl with him, who he assumed was Maria. Anthony's mood had changed completely from the almost deliriously giddy guy who had shown Bodie out, earlier that evening, the hours of worry had worn him down; and Bodie and Maria didn't look much happier.

Anthony looked for Dan, outside on the drive, then back enquiringly at Bodie. 'We heard about the attack on the West End. It didn't come near you, did it?' Bodie slowly nodded. 'Dan?' Bodie shook his head, grimly. Anthony shut the door.

It was devastating news, which a pale Lily also took in, as she came from the living room. She had been crying most of the evening, and she burst into tears again, setting Maria off.

Bodie hugged Maria, while Anthony took Lily in his arms.

'We've lost Dan?' whimpered Lily, who would have collapsed if not for Anthony's arms. 'Bodie, I'm so sorry. I'm so, so sorry.'

'He took a terrorist with him,' said Bodie. 'He protected me and Maria.'

Lily gasped. It was all becoming very real, all of a sudden. She managed to control herself, and looked at the girl: her love rival. Maria seemed to be in shock, not at all concerned to find these strangers in her house.

'You must be Maria,' said Lily, stating the obvious. Maria nodded, without looking. Her eyes were glassy. Lily took Maria's hand and led her through to the kitchen.

Bodie went into the living room with Anthony, and they both sat down. Mrs Cowfield had gone to bed. The television was off. The silence buzzed in Bodie's ears like tinnitus.

'Tell me, was it really bad?' asked Anthony.

'It was sudden, and noisy, and terrifying. We were lucky, me and Maria.'

'At least you got her. Have you told her the big picture?'

'Yes, we had a long talk in her car. The worst chat of my life. I think she heard me, but maybe, in the morning, she'll ask a lot of questions.'

'You need some sleep, mate.'

Bodie rubbed his head. 'Yes. I'll have some food, then crash for a few hours. Wake me as soon as you want to get going. Where's the Professor?'

Lily and Maria came in, carrying cups of tea; the staple requirement for all English distress. They sat together on the sofa. Lily had clearly decided to take care of Maria.

'There was an incident, while you were away,' said Anthony, then went on to explain the Professor Siddiq situation to Bodie.

Bodie didn't know what to say. He had become quite attached to the Professor. He knew that Lily liked the man, too. 'So, what, we push on without him?' he finally said.

'No!' said Lily, indignant. 'No, we can't go without him.'

'He's in police custody, baby,' said Bodie. He realised that he had called her baby. 'Lily, what can we do? Break him out of jail?'

'Why not? You've got guns.'

Bodie thought about that for a moment, then wiped a hand across his face. 'Oh, my God.'

Bodie looked at Anthony. Anthony was looking at Maria. He bore her no animosity for being the cause of Dan's untimely death. She seemed a nice, normal English girl. He turned his gaze to Bodie.

'Let's think about this, Bodie,' said Anthony. 'He was just involved in a fracas. They might just bail him in the morning.'

'They'll put his name through the computer first. Then he'll be handed over, in due course.'

'We're short of time. I don't think we can sit and wait for him, even if they don't run a check and just kick him out in the morning. And, as for going in to get him... risk versus reward. We should go on without him.'

'No!' shouted Lily. 'Salman put this all into focus for you two guys. No, we mustn't leave him to die.'

Maria started to shake, so Lily held her.

Bodie stood, needing sustenance. He was so proud of his Lily. He smiled at her, then squeezed his cousin's shoulder. 'Anthony, mate. Better find out where the nearest police station is.'

It had gone dark, and Brian and Vivienne Rhodes were stuck in a motorway tailback, trying to get to Southampton, and from there, a ferry to the Isle of Wight. Vivienne had put a travelling blanket over them both and was snuggled in to her husband. Hours ago, they had argued about the situation, apportioning blame for the decision to go, then tried to find a way to abort the trip, but they were so far away from an off ramp, that they were, basically, stuffed. It was the kind of situation that they saw on the news, from time to time, but usually in bad Winter weather - members of the public (idiots trying to get from Aberdeen to Inverness in a blizzard) stranded overnight in their cars, or walked out by the police to a nearby Scout hut, or something similar.

Luckily, they had an emergency supply of snacks and water, and as the hours went by, they just relaxed into the situation, hoping that whatever the trouble was, up ahead, it would eventually be cleared and they could either move on, or turn back for home.

'Oh, Brian, we should have emigrated to Australia last year, when we had the chance.'

'It's only a traffic jam, sweetheart. It's not the end of the world.'

She giggled. 'All right, I'll imagine us back skiing in Verbier.'

'Queuing for the ski lift?'

'No, silly. I'm just sending my mind to a nicer place.'

'What could be nicer than being here with me?'

'Of course, honey. Oh, your mother rang yesterday...'

'I do apologise about that.'

'Shush.' She slapped his arm. 'She says there are tiles coming free from the roof.'

'I shall deal with it, if we ever get home again.'

'I've decided to re-do the downstairs loo. I've called that plumber man you don't rate.'

'As you wish.'

'And your mother said that your Auntie Susan is going ahead with that keyhole surgery thing on her vein.'

'I should think so, as well. It's a very simple procedure.'

'And I'm pregnant.'


Anthony and Bodie left the Cowfield house at about 3 a.m. Both Lily and Maria were asleep. Anthony wondered what the neighbours made of all the comings and goings, and he was highly concerned about approaching a police station at such an ungodly hour.

After a *Google* search, they had discovered that they could actually walk to the nearest police station, even though there was no guarantee of Professor Siddiq even being there. But the die was cast, they were going to give it a go.

As they walked, Bodie described the events in the restaurant. Anthony was extremely proud of Bodie's actions to end the situation, but held his tongue. Bodie was concerned about how he would break the news to Dan's parents, before

Anthony reminded him that he wouldn't actually have to.

'Modern police stations,' mused Bodie. 'They're not like *Dixon of Dock Green*, any more. They've closed most of them, and I don't know what the procedure is during the night.'

Anthony mulled that over. 'It's a twenty-four hour police service, so there must be officers in there. Or at least some support staff.'

'What do we do? Ring the front door bell?'

'We'll play it by ear.'

They had swapped guns in the lounge, as Bodie's was now empty, and Anthony felt like bowing to his young cousin's new, extra experience. He would still wave his empty weapon around, if the need arose.

In the end, they needn't have worried about how to gain access to the police station, as a police van pulled up alongside them and two officers stepped out. They were big units: one white, with a shaven-head, called PC Reed, the other of mixed-race, called PC Glover.

'All right, lads?' asked PC Reed. 'Where are you off to, at this time of the morning?'

Anthony felt like playing games, continuing to creep forward, so that PC Reed had to block his path.

'Steady now,' said PC Reed. 'Don't make me have to cuff you. We've had a report of an assault. That's why we stopped you.'

Anthony scratched his beard, turned his head to the side and looked closely at PC Reed. 'Do you know you're about to die?'

PC Glover stepped nearer, but still allowed his colleague to do all the talking.

'Now play nice,' PC Reed said to Anthony. 'Where are you going? It's a simple question.'

Bodie couldn't take any more. He drew his hand gun, but he hadn't counted on the speed of PC Glover's reaction, and suddenly they were wrestling madly on the floor. Anthony had no time to take his own gun out before PC Reed was trying to get him in a head lock. Anthony punched upwards, hitting the stab vest three times before he connected with the officer's chin. Then they were grappling alongside the other two, legs and arms going everywhere, like a bad game of *Twister*.

It was an even fight between Bodie and Glover, but eventually Bodie managed to get the muzzle of his gun up under the policeman's chin. Once they stopped wrestling, the other two realised what had happened, and Anthony was able to kneel up and bring out his gun. Everyone was short of breath.

'Don't be silly now,' was all PC Glover could say.

'Be quiet,' replied Bodie. 'Take off your handcuffs. Put one on you, and one on your mate.' Reluctantly, the policemen complied. 'Now, listen. We don't want to hurt you. We just want our friend out of your custody. You are going to take us in, give him to us, and we will leave without firing a shot. Is that understood? Is that understood!?'

'Yes, son,' answered PC Reed. 'Stay calm.'

Anthony took keys from PC Reed. He had some experience of policing, from his previous journalistic research. He would make the officers sit up front, with he and Bodie in the back, but with the connecting metal gate open, to keep them covered. Once in the police yard, they could all exit through the front of the vehicle, and hopefully gain entry to the station.

Bodie kept the policemen covered, while Anthony jumped in the cab and unlocked the mesh gate. Bodie got in next, beckoning the policemen to follow him as he backed in.

'Are you sure you want to do this, son?' asked PC Reed.

'Shut up.'

Within a minute, they were driving to the station, PC Glover's shackled right hand having to move alongside PC Reed's left, as the gears were changed. Bodie sat close, aiming his gun. Anthony relaxed back against the inner wall of the van, sighing. Then he jumped out of his skin to realise that there was an actual prisoner already in there.

'What!? What!?' enquired Bodie, without looking.

'They've already got a geezer in here.'

Despite the seriousness of the event, PC Reed laughed. 'That's Arthur. Arthur, meet two future lifers.'

Anthony looked at an elderly man in the gloom of the back of the van. He looked like a tramp, and he smelled of booze and urine. 'All right?'

Arthur did not respond, just stared with rheumy eyes at the odd happenings.

'We won't harm you,' said Anthony. 'You just stay sitting there, okay?'

Arthur offered Anthony something from a white bag. 'Have a sweet.'

'No, thank you.'

'Have a sweet.'

'No, really, I'm good. Thank you.'

'Have a bloody sweet!'

To keep the peace, Anthony looked in the bag, saw Mint Humbugs, mimed that he was happy to see those, picked one out and made a big show of popping it into his mouth.

'That's been up my bum,' said Arthur.

Sergeant John Clark was standing against the open cell door, having a cup of tea with his prisoner, Professor Siddiq. He had forty years in the police service, and thought he had heard it all in that time. He was bald, with heavy lines in his forehead, a scar on his left eyebrow from being glassed, and one of those mouths that naturally turned downwards, although he was by no means a miserable person.

'Well, Professor, that's been fascinating to listen to. So, we're all going to be dead by Monday? At least that gets me off my double shift. Was the tea all right for you?'

Professor Siddiq passed back his mug. 'It was very nice, thank you, Sergeant.'

'Will there be anything else? A pillow? An extra blanket?'

Professor Siddiq was happy to play out the police sarcasm pantomime. 'I don't think so.'

There came the sound of the outside door to the Custody suite being opened.

'It sounds like you're having company, Professor. You must tell them your story, too.'

With that, he locked the cell and wandered back to his front desk, yawning widely. It was time for a few Drunk and Disorderlies to be brought in. Looking through the bars of the connecting door, he saw PC's Reed and Glover bringing in three prisoners. He hit the switch to open the door, then stood to reach for one of his favourite Garibaldi biscuits.

Next thing he knew, he had the two officers kneeling below his desk, handcuffed together and looking like they had been in a fight.

'What the hell?'

'Shut it!' shouted Anthony, aiming his empty gun. 'Get down here. Now!'

Sergeant Clark cursed under his breath, if he had been in his seat he could have hit the silent alarm; as it was, his worst nightmare was happening without the hope of back-up. He moved around the desk and was made to kneel beside the others.

'We want the Professor,' said Bodie.

'Why would you want him?' asked Sergeant Clark.

'Where is he!?'

'In cell Number Two.'

'Keys?'

'On my belt.'

Anthony lunged forward to unclip the keys. All Sergeant Clark could think about was his disciplinary hearing, his shame for letting it happen, his possible loss of pension; it all rushed around his brain with the hot blood, and he made a grab for Anthony's gun.

'No, Sarge!' shouted PC Reed.

Anthony fought back, trying not to hurt the older man. But Clark was a bull of a man and easily overturned Anthony. He had the gun free, was grappling to get his hand on the butt. Bodie knew the gun was empty, knew the Desk Sergeant was a man who probably had grandchildren, but also knew and believed in what was to happen, so he aimed his own weapon and shot the Sergeant once through the left temple.

Once the metallic bang had stopped reverberating around the austere room, all that was left was the smell of the discharge and the shock of everyone there.

PC Glover was enraged, wanting to get up, but his wiser colleague stopped him. Anthony took the keys and staggered to the row of cells. The Professor's name was written on a whiteboard above the second door. He unlocked it, looked in, and saw the most relieved pair of eyes that he had ever seen.

PC's Reed and Glover, the latter swearing his head off, were then locked in the cell, before the three of them escaped the police station. It seemed to make sense to take the police van. Professor Siddiq climbed through to the back, with Bodie and Anthony up front. Bodie backed them out, and they were soon on the road, heading back to the Cowfield house.

'Have a sweet,' said Arthur to Professor Siddiq.

# 21

The Webb group were stuck in the same motorway traffic jam as Dr and Mrs Rhodes, on the M3 leading down to Southampton, but they knew the cause of the hold-up: that the people were not as stupid as the politicians thought they were.

Wendy Webb wanted to punch and scratch her way through all the people to get to the ferry. She now believed her husband's conspiracy theory entirely. She was also getting hungry again, reaching for her secret stash of *Jaffa Cakes* in the door pocket.

'Hey, Mum!' shouted Kirk, spotting her actions. 'Share.'

'Get lost.'

Rageh Abdi, increasingly despondent in the rear seat, pushed Kirk in the shoulder. 'Please don't shout.'

Kirk spun around, angrily, 'Are you looking to lose your front teeth?'

Steven punched his brother's arm, 'You disturbed me, as well, you dick.'

The VW van engine was switched on, as the traffic started to crawl forward.

'No fighting,' said David. 'See, we're moving again.'

Daniel Berbatov was almost comatose, sitting in the direct sunshine. "English pigs" he mimed at Rageh.

Rageh tried to buck himself up. He slapped Daniel's knee. 'See, all the people trying to get there, it proves my point.'

'I bow to your greater intelligence.'

'The last motorway sign said five miles to Southampton.'

'That could be one day for each mile.'

'Come on, what's the plan for when we get there?'

'Rageh, the ferries will be full.'

'We'll find a boat.'

'Well, let me sleep now, so I will have energy for the search. But, listen...' He lowered his voice. 'As soon as we get there, we lose these people.'

Rageh nodded enthusiastically. 'You sleep, Daniel. You sleep.'

At Newbury, Ari and Sarah got up early, packed small travelling bags and then had a quick breakfast of cereals and tea in the kitchen. Overnight, Sarah had made a few phone calls, but nobody in her sphere of influence had an answer as to why MPs and their families were being gathered up. Obviously, terrorism was hinted at, but there was no clear evidence. And... why the Isle of Wight?

She moved in for a kiss and a cuddle, safe as always against his strong chest. 'I love you, Ari.'

'I love you, too.'

A vehicle crunched over their gravel drive. They saw that it was a police Land Rover. A sole policeman got out. While Ari locked the back door, Sarah introduced them.

'I'm Sergeant Sykes. Very nice to meet you.'

Handshakes all round. The Sergeant loaded their bags, they climbed in, and headed off to the unknown rendezvous.

'Do you think it will it take us long, Sergeant?' asked Sarah.

'I believe the motorways are busy, Ma'am. But we can always blue light it down the hard shoulder, have no fear. I'm surprised they didn't fly you over in a chopper.'

'I suppose they couldn't do that for all six hundred and fifty Members of Parliament, and their spouses, and children.'

'What?' Sergeant Sykes looked at her in his rear view mirror. 'All MPs are going there?' It seemed to confirm all the things that had been worrying him.

Over the centuries, the Isle of Wight has had thousands of shipwrecks on its coast. The town of Ventnor, in the south of the island, has had its fair share.

The Jordan family had just sold their six-bedroom detached home, overlooking the sea, at Ventnor, for £1.3m. They had enjoyed the house enormously for the last six years, but they were relocating to Dubai, due to Jim Jordan's work in the construction industry. Jim, his wife, Elaine, and their two young daughters, Grace and Francesca had been packing their belongings for the last couple of days, and all had been looking out to sea occasionally, trying to imprint the image on their memories. Normally, they only saw sailing craft playing about off shore, or the occasional tanker, on the horizon. On that particular, clear morning they had the extraordinary sight of a stranded cruise ship on the beach, as tall as an apartment building. The Jordans stood on their verandah to take in the scene.

Army helicopters were overhead, which wasn't a surprise, given that the Prime Minister was reported to be on the island. The RNLI lifeboat crews were in attendance, but there seemed no great risk to life. Passengers and crew were disembarking from the rear gangway and gathering on the sand.

'Come on, ladies,' called Mr Jordan. 'Let's finish the bedrooms, and then we can have some brunch.'

'But, Dad...' appealed Grace, opening her hands to the once in a lifetime view.

'It's not going anywhere, darling. Come on, the moving lorry is coming tomorrow, remember.'

'Talking about lorries,' said Elaine, as two Army trucks and three coaches came along the road. 'Wouldn't have thought they needed all those. I read that most passengers got off, soon after the terrorist attack.'

'Yes,' said Jim. 'The "frightened to fly brigade" still on board, just like you.'

'I'm flying to the Middle East, aren't I? I must love you.'

The convoy stopped at the row of houses below the Jordan property. Police and Coastguard officials disembarked. They began knocking on doors. Jim Jordan watched, a little puzzled, then insisted that his family get on with the task at hand.

An hour later, while having croissants and juice for brunch, the family moved outside to catch up on the rescue scene. They were just in time to see a policeman coming up their drive.

'Hello there,' called Jim.

'Hello, sir. I'm Police Constable Hamer.'

He indicated the ship. 'Not every day we see that kind of thing.'

'I'm sure. Is it Mr Jordan? I have an official letter for you, sir.'

Jim turned to Elaine. 'Take the girls inside, Elaine.'

Mrs Jordan did as she was asked.

'It's all a bit odd, this, PC Hamer.'

'Read that, sir, if you would.'

Jim Jordan read the official government letter, which requested that he and his family were to comply with all police directions, and to board one of the buses, with minimal luggage, to be conveyed to the new Eco-City, outside the capital, Newport. He looked up into the face of the policeman.

'What on earth is this? It's like being interned, during the Second World War. You can't be serious? We're moving out tomorrow.'

'I have to tell you, Mr Jordan, if you refuse to comply willingly with the orders in that document, then you and your family will be arrested.'

'What!?'

'It's just my orders, sir. Are you going to get ready?'

Jim was red in the face with apoplexy. Then he looked out at the ship.

'What's on that ship, officer?'

'Pardon, sir?'

'What's on that ship? Is it a dirty bomb, or something?'

PC Hamer looked down to the beach. 'I wouldn't know, sir.'

Jim Jordan could see it now; terrorists were trying to take a boat containing a dirty bomb, in to wherever the Prime Minister was having his "conference" or whatever it was. They were just protecting local residents while they dealt with it. Thank God his house sale had been completed. All that mattered was his family's safety.

'How long have we got, PC Hamer?'

'If you could be ready within thirty minutes, sir.'

'We'll be ready.'


'It just gets worse,' said Margaret Fallon, as she and Barry came carefully down the gangway and set foot back on English soil. They had already been told that it was the Isle of Wight. Barry shaded his eyes and looked up at the hulking ship, which had finally lost its battle in the early hours of the morning and drifted ashore.

'It reminds me of Isambard Kingdom Brunels's *Great Eastern*, right now.'

'More like the *Titanic*, in my opinion, Barry. Oh, look, there's our favourite steward, Ravi.'

Margaret went over to the Indian steward, who was still in his high-buttoned white jacket. He politely smiled. He had been musing over his vanishing gratuities.

'Hello, Mrs Fallon.'

'Ravi. What a to-do. Do you know what's happening?

Nobody is telling us anything.'

'I believe the coaches are to take us inland.'

'And from there, across to the mainland?'

'I would assume so.'

'Thank you, Ravi. Oh, this is for you.' She handed him an envelope full of cash.

'Thank you. Thank you, Mr and Mrs Fallon. I wish you a safe journey home.'

'I hope things work out for you, too,' said Barry, shaking the steward's hand.

'I wanted to change ships, anyway,' joked Ravi.

They moved off to be near the other, small number of passengers. Before they could take part in the gossip or general complaining, the Purser gathered them to him and started to lead them up the beach to a coach. In all the confusion, no-one realised that they were sharing the coach with local residents. The Fallons sat there in just the clothes they had on; all possessions lost, survivors of a terrorist attack, limping home on a damaged ship, then shipwrecked within sight of their home port. Now to be shuttled around on a coach. They were very tired. Happily, they accepted sandwiches and cartons of orange juice being passed back.

After about half an hour, the Fallons heard the coach engine start up with a growl.

'We're off,' said Margaret, patting Barry's leg.

She looked left, as a family came on to the coach and sat themselves down.

'What a palaver,' she said to them.

Elaine Jordan replied, 'Yes, isn't it just.'

'I don't remember seeing you on board ship.'

'That's because we weren't. We live here in Ventnor.'

Oh, thought Margaret, sharing the coach with non-passengers. 'Not even given our own coach,' she whispered to Barry. 'Put that on the compensation list.'

They set off, everyone watching the beached ship, until the coach turned away. Soon, they were rushing along quiet country lanes. The people on the left side of the bus seemed, to Margaret, to all be locals, who kept chatting to each other, while all the ship passengers just sat quietly or slept.

After a relatively short drive, the coach slowed onto a private road, and took up station behind a line of other coaches. All the people were straining to see what was going on. Gradually, the coach eased forward, as each one was checked by military personnel - military personnel with machine-guns, Margaret noticed. As the coach moved through a specially designed series of air-tight locks, Margaret started to become distressed, and got to her feet.

'What is going on here?' asked Margaret. 'Can someone please tell me?'

Elaine Jordan reached out to hold her hand. 'Don't you know? We're being taken into the Eco-Town that's been built on the island. The Prime Minister and the Cabinet are here. There's some kind of emergency going on.'

'*What?*'

'There might be a dirty bomb on that stranded ship,' suggested Jim. 'But we'll be safe in here. It's all air-conditioned.'

Margaret turned to Barry. Other passengers were standing

up, with cruise staff trying to reassure them.

When the coach was guided into a parking spot, all the passengers were allowed to step down. It was very bright inside the dome, with natural sunlight, but it definitely felt like being underground. The entire sky was opaque, slightly grey. There was no wind, just a pleasant ambient temperature. Looking about, from their elevated position, the area seemed to be as big as looking into a real valley. Extraordinary that it was all a totally sealed environment.

Nearby, there were modern, tightly compacted buildings, but with a lot of trees and shrubs. It was an extremely calm and pleasant place to be.

'You're safe here,' Jim said to Margaret, before turning to hug his family.

Margaret turned to Barry, at a loss for words.

'Well, dear,' said Barry, holding her. 'At least it's a holiday to remember.'

# 22

Arthur the tramp had been given some cash, for a square meal and some new sweets, and then abandoned, along with the police van, around the corner from the Cowfield residence.

Bodie, Anthony and Professor Siddiq walked the rest of the way. They decided to let the girls sleep on a little longer. While they waited for the sun to come up, they made coffee and toast in the kitchen.

Professor Siddiq had already thanked them profusely. His despair at the behaviour recently of some of his fellow human beings had been eased by the selfless acts of his two friends. He was terribly sorry to hear about Dan, but keen to meet Maria.

'We'll take Mr Cowfield's car,' said Anthony. 'We'll forget

the Galaxy now.'

'What car is it?' asked Bodie.

Anthony slightly pulled a face. 'Porsche Cayenne. Very sweet.'

'Then why pull a face at it?'

'Just, the headcase who was running the smuggling ring in Sheffield; he drove one. That's all. It will be great.' He spread marmalade on his toast. 'So, a quick burn to Newbury, then straight down to Southampton. I was looking at the news earlier, there's extra traffic heading south. Looks like some people have figured it out for themselves.'

'Do you think we will make it?' asked Professor Siddiq, eating ravenously. 'I'm just worried, that's all. I'm not suggesting we don't try for Lily's family.'

'You'd better not,' joked Bodie. 'Lily's not in the mood for leaving anyone behind.'

They left it another hour, then Bodie went to wake the girls. He found them sleeping together, in their clothes, on a double bed in a back bedroom. He realised that he was unsure which ex-girlfriend to wake first, so bounced his knees on the bottom of the bed, and they both gradually stirred.

'Hey, time to go,' he said.

'Bodie!' called Lily. 'You're safe.' She bounded over the bed to embrace him. 'Did you get Salman?'

'Yes, he's downstairs.'

'You did!! Yay!'

Maria sat up and smiled at him.

'Right,' said Bodie. 'You two girls do... whatever it is you girls need to do, because we're going in exactly ten minutes.'

'*Ten minutes?*' asked Lily, teasing.

'Yes, so, hustle, hustle. Come on.'

He sat himself down on the bed, crossing his legs, pretending that he was going to watch them get ready. Both girls laughed and pushed him, despite his mock protestations, out of the bedroom.

Maria came down first, in ripped jeans and a grey top. She was introduced to Professor Siddiq, and then she set about quickly making some breakfast for herself, Lily and Mrs Cowfield, still in bed.

Anthony got the Porsche out of the double garage. Bodie packed some supplies into the boot. Lily came downstairs and threw herself into Professor Siddiq's arms. They hugged until Maria forced a plate of crumpets between them.

'I'll just take this to my gran,' said Maria, taking a tray upstairs.

Maria went into her grandmother's bedroom and gently woke her.

'Gran, good morning. I'm going out now with my friends. Is that okay?'

'Yes, sweetheart. You have a lovely time.'

'There's some toast and tea there. Mrs Dawson will be here later, remember. You enjoy your day at the Bingo.'

'Yes, dear.'

Maria leant over and tenderly kissed her grandmother for the very last time. 'I love you, Gran.'

Outside the bedroom, Maria put a hand to her mouth, distraught. She would never see her grandmother ever again. She didn't cry until she was downstairs, closing the front door and getting into her dad's car, with the others.

'Not far now until we get off the motorway, honey,' Dr Rhodes tried to reassure his wife.

They were moving a few yards every minute. He smiled at her, still unable to stop smiling at the news of her pregnancy.

Sarah sighed. 'Whatever is going on, Brian? It's not the holidays. Why is everyone trying to get to Southampton? Is there a boat show on, do you think?'

'I don't know, darling.'

'It's a good job I have my own business. Think of the people in this queue who are trying to get to work. I wonder what some of them do for a living.'

'Shall we create a new game? Guess the career of the people from the state of the car?'

Brian laughed.

'Don't be cruel, Brian.'

'The people in the fifteen year old Skoda are dog valeters.'

'Brian!'

'It says it, on the back. Now, look at that couple, in the old BMW X3. He's a builder, and she's... oh, she looks stern, she's one of those order pickers in a supermarket. You know, the ones who get in the way.'

'You and your pet hates.'

'The weather is staying nice, anyway.'

Since the Wembley tornado, he had been monitoring the skies religiously. Vivienne, rested her hand on his left thigh.

'Something good is coming from this trip,' she told him.

'What's that?'

'All these gear changes are firming up your thigh.'

Sergeant Sykes had made good time along the M3 motorway in his police Land Rover. Only when they were nearing Southampton did the traffic slow to a crawl, so he immediately put on his *Blues and Twos* and took to the hard shoulder.

Ari and Sarah felt like Royalty, as they watched frustrated faces stare at them as they went by. They held hands. They were becoming increasingly nervous.

'Not long now,' called back Sergeant Sykes.

'Thank you,' answered Sarah. 'I didn't ask, where are you from, Sergeant Sykes?'

'I'm a Portsmouth lad,' said the Sergeant. He then had to negotiate a vehicle that was straying onto the hard shoulder. He gave the driver a dirty look. 'But I'm based in Newport, on the island, Ma'am. So, I'll be going home after delivering you. It's my daughter's fifth birthday today.'

'Is it? How lovely.'

'Yes, I've got her a...whoooahh!'

A shocking smash happened to the Land Rover, with Sergeant Sykes braking hard, glass absolutely everywhere, with Sarah screaming in shock. The windshield had come in. The noise and the air was dreadful, until Sergeant Sykes managed to bring the vehicle to a stop. Ari checked that his wife was all right, then looked ahead to the policeman. There was a lump of concrete sitting on top of the buckled steering wheel. Sergeant Sykes had blood coming from his hands, but seemed lucky to be alive.

'Are you okay, Sergeant?' asked Ari.

'Yes, thank you, sir. Some kids dropped a lump of concrete on us from a bridge. Unbelievable. It could have killed me.'

They all got out. Sarah inspected Sergeant Sykes's wounds. There was a First Aid kit on the passenger side of the dashboard, so she made him sit down, while she looked in the box.

Dr and Mrs Rhodes had watched the police Land Rover pass them with mutual contempt and annoyance, then both gasped, as the concrete slab fell from the bridge, right onto it, glass spraying upwards as if it were a bomb going off. Immediately, Dr Rhodes pulled his car onto the hard shoulder and drove up behind the stationary police vehicle. He told Vivienne to stay in the car, took his Doctor's bag from the back seat and ran forward.

He would not have been surprised to find fatalities, so was relieved to see one policeman having his wounds tended to by a woman.

'Excuse me, I'm a doctor. Let me there, please.'

Sarah was happy to defer to the professional, turning to be held by Ari.

'You've been very lucky,' Dr Rhodes told Sergeant Sykes. 'I'll do what I can. You will have to go to hospital. A couple of fingers are broken.'

'Thanks, Doctor. I'll call for back-up.'

Dr Rhodes looked back at Ari and Sarah. 'Anybody else hurt?'

'No, we're fine,' said Ari. 'Thank you for your help.'

Dr Rhodes helped Sergeant Sykes use his radio, then stood

away to speak to the Fransiscas. 'Should I know you?'

'No, I suppose not,' answered Ari. 'I'm Ari, and this is my wife, Sarah. Sarah's an MP, that's why the police were taking us to Southampton.'

'I'm Brian. What's the big rush to Southampton? The world seems to have gone mad.'

'There's an emergency developing. We assume it must be terrorist related.'

'Well, that would explain it. Errm, what are you going to do now? Wait for help to come?'

'I don't know.'

'We're only a mile from the end of the motorway. You could come with my wife and I. Or..?'

Ari conferred with Sarah, and they both looked to Sergeant Sykes.

'I'm okay,' said Sergeant Sykes. 'If you want to go on with this gentleman and his wife. I don't know how long we would have to wait here.'

'Then, we'll come with you, Brian,' said Ari. 'Thank you.'

Both Ari and Sarah thanked Sergeant Sykes, while Dr Rhodes left him with some painkillers. Ari collected their bags, and then they went back to the Rhodes's car. Vivienne was introduced, while Dr Rhodes edged them back into the traffic.

'That was an awful thing to happen,' said Vivienne. 'Are you sure you're both all right.'

'Yes, thank you,' replied Sarah. 'So, why are you two going to Southampton?'

'The plan was for a little rest,' said Vivienne. 'We have a property near Ryde, you see. But we'll need a proper holiday after all this nonsense.'

The emergency was discussed, as they crawled along. There came a little spurt in the movement of the traffic, and they were off the motorway sooner than expected. Dr Rhodes drove them down the still busy A-road into the city of Southampton.

Anthony was driving the Porsche Cayenne at high speed along the M4 motorway towards Newbury. It would take less than an hour. Professor Siddiq was alongside him, trying to find a decent radio station. Lily was asleep, while Bodie chatted with Maria.

'How are we for ammunition, Bodie?' asked Anthony.

'I'm not an expert, but I'd say I've got two bullets. And we have the tasers.'

Bodie returned to sharing looks with Maria.

'What?' he asked.

'Bodie, you brought your girlfriend with you, when you came to save me.'

'Yes... I did.'

'In any other situation, that would be considered very odd. Anyway, Lily is so, so sweet. You're an idiot for finishing with her.'

'Thank you.'

She took his hand. 'I thought about you often, you know.'

'Me, too.'

'Do you think we'll get through this?'

'Hey, look at the team you're on. We'll get Lily's brother, and then storm the ferry port.'

'He should punch you on the nose, for mistreating his

sister. And then kiss you for saving her.'

'What a situation, huh? You know, Maria, when this is all over, do you think we could try again?'

'I'd like that. I can't imagine what we'll be coming out to, but I want to be with you.'

They kissed gently and snuggled in together, until Lily stirred, and Maria pushed him off.

'Show respect to Lily,' she whispered. 'We're not an item again until after all this.'

'You're right, of course.'

Lily rubbed her eyes and looked at Bodie.

'Hello, sleepy head,' he said.

'Where are we?'

'Almost at your brother's place.'

'Yay!'

Every road into the Southampton ferry terminals was clogged with traffic. Horns were being blared. Many people were leaving their vehicles and walking in. There were helicopters above and a heavy security presence on the ground. The chaos was very disheartening to the people in the Rhodes car. By that stage, Dr Rhodes and Vivienne were keen to get across to the island; it was a primal urge to escape danger. Dr Rhodes saw a fluorescent uniform alongside his window, so opened it and spoke to a female police officer.

'Excuse me, excuse me, officer. Can you help us?'

'Sorry, sir, it's best if you turn around and go home.'

'Please, we have an MP here with us, we are supposed to deliver her as soon as possible. It's Sarah...'

'...Fransisca-Smith,' put in Sarah, from the back seat.

'...Sarah Francisca-Smith, officer.'

The WPC spoke into her shoulder radio, then waited for a reply. She cocked her head to hear the garbled reply, then looked down at Dr Rhodes. 'You have to leave the car, and all come with me, right this second.'

'Okay, okay,' said Dr Rhodes.

The four of them grabbed their bags and rushed to follow the small WPC , who was a tough cookie, barging a path for them through the crowds. She led them to a cordoned off area, spoke with the armed police officers who stood guard there, and they passed through a gate into a calmer zone. They walked across a car-park. Through a mesh fence, to the side, they were able to see the hordes of desperate people queuing to try to pay for a ferry.

A more senior policeman came towards them and relieved the WPC.

'I'm Inspector Callaghan,' he introduced himself, touching the peak of his cap. 'Mrs Fransisca-Smith?'

'Yes, that's me,' said Sarah.

'I'm glad you could make it. You're cutting it fine.' He shook everyone's hand. 'Follow me, please.'

They were led further into the complex, into a building, and across a glass walkway, through which they could see a red and white ferry, apparently about to depart.

'I'm with the local boys,' said Inspector Callaghan. 'I'm going to hand you over to the Metropolitan team who have taken over here. They will take you onwards.'

'Thank you, Inspector Callaghan,' said Sarah. She had taken

on a more serious demeanour. 'Do you know what this is all about?'

'I could hazard a guess, Ma'am. Here we are. Let me speak to them first.'

They had come in at the side of a massive queue to the ferry reception area. There were police with their machine-guns everywhere. The noise was intense. They watched as the Inspector spoke to officials on the desk, who looked over. The Inspector came back.

'They want you two first,' said Inspector Callaghan, indicating the Rhodes. 'I would suggest they want to turn you away if you are not island residents.'

'Oh, but we own property there,' said Vivienne.

'Can you prove that? It's very important that you can.'

Vivienne rooted about in her handbag. 'I think so, yes.'

'Very good. Well, off you go.'

Dr Rhodes and Vivienne turned to Ari and Sarah, exchanging hugs and best wishes.

Ari and Sarah held each other. There was a fight going on nearby. The noise was bringing a tear to Sarah's eye. It was all such a terrible scene. She thought about family members. She thought about her constituents. Ari made her watch the Rhodes. They were proving that they owned a property on the island, and then they were given a stamped document and allowed to pass through. They both looked back and waved. Ari and Sarah waved enthusiastically.

'Go forward, please' said Inspector Callaghan. 'Best of luck to you.'

'Thank you, Inspector,' said Ari.

Inspector Callaghan left them. Ari guided his wife forward to the frantically waving official.

'Are you Mrs Fransisca-Smith, MP?' asked the man behind the desk, reading off a clipboard.

A big woman in the queue was screaming that she was next in line. Sarah could see her in her peripheral vision, but did not dare look at her properly.

'Yes, I am, and this is my husband, Ari Fransisca.'

'Proof, please? Driver's licence, something like that?'

They both came up with required proof of identity. Ari hugged Sarah. She smiled up at him.

'Soon be over,' he said to her ear, and squeezed her tighter.

The officials nodded at their ID's. 'Mrs Fransisca-Smith, if you would come this way, please. But I'm afraid this gentleman is denied access.'

'I beg your pardon?' asked Sarah.

'I only have your name on my list, Madam.'

'But this is my husband. I can vouch for him.'

'I'm sorry, Madam. I have my instructions. Please come through, the last ferry is about to depart.'

'No! I'm not going without my husband. Get me your superior, right now!'

'There is no time, Madam. Look at that clock, you have one minute to get down that gangway. Please...'

Sarah was as devastated, as Ari was dumbfounded. The official had people trying to get over the counter. Armed police were moving in.

'Darling!' said Ari, grasping Sarah's arms. 'You must go now. You must. You have to go without me.'

'No. No. Ari, I refuse to. Ari...'

'Darling, it's clearly not safe here. I need you to go for that ferry.'

Ari was physically moving his wife away from him.

'Madam!?' implored the official.

Sarah made the decision, as definitely as if she had stamped her foot. 'No.' With that, she lost her face in her beloved Ari's chest, the desk was overrun, warning shots were fired, and the order was given for the last ferry to depart.

# 23

Wendy Webb and her two sons punched and kicked the officials on the ferry check-in desk until warning gunshots rang out. A wave of bodies flooded away from the entrance, and then started to dissipate in abject misery, back out onto the car-parks.

Daniel and Rageh were equally distraught. Panic ran through their veins and they began to seriously think about dying, for the first time. Having Kirk and Steven Webb near to them was, by then, simply intolerable, and they both lashed out. The Webb boys fought back, leading to a wild fist fight, amidst horrified members of the public.

David Webb managed to get his bulk between the warring foursome. 'Listen. Listen to me! I have a plan. Daniel, Rageh, stay with us, be cool. I know how to get through this. I know where to go.'

The situation cooled. Daniel, a bump coming up on his left eyebrow, looked at Rageh. Rageh, with a split lip, looked at Daniel. What else were they going to do?

The traffic attempting to leave Southampton was quite heavy, too. The VW Camper van moved along in second gear. The Webb boys were still in fairly mutinous mood, and when they saw a train track running beside the road, Kirk suggested to his brother that they get a train back to Essex.

The traffic came to a halt. Wendy was less than happy; all the travelling, the stress, and the activity made her feel like she was on a dual diet and exercise purge. 'What's the delay now?' She looked ahead three vehicles, to a mini-bus sitting under a railway bridge, with traffic flowing the other way. There seemed to be no obstruction in front of the mini-bus. 'Another cretin. Beep your horn, David.'

David Webb hesitated, so Wendy did it for him. Still the mini-bus loitered.

'Stephen, Kirk, go and see,' ordered Wendy.

Both replied, 'Are you joking?'

Wendy huffed, then heaved her size from the van and walked forward. She looked daggers at the people in the cars behind the mini-bus, as if it were more their responsibility, then banged on the side window and looked in. There was only the driver, a bearded Asian man.

'Oi!' shouted Wendy. 'Have you broken down?'

The driver continued to look forward, totally ignoring

Wendy. She slapped her hand on the window again, infuriated. Then, incensed at being ignored, she looked about for something to attack the mini-bus with, a brick or a length of wood, but finding nothing, she had to retreat back to the van, hauling herself back in.

'Has he broken down?' asked David.

'It's an Asian bloke. Refused to even look at me. Probably can't speak English.'

Rageh and Daniel decided to go and see. They walked down quickly, but they got the same treatment.

'What's he doing?' asked Daniel. 'Having a nervous breakdown, or something?'

Rageh scratched his beard. Then he heard the train coming, and the situation became crystal clear to him. He looked at Daniel, and the same realisation had just hit him.

'Run,' said Daniel.

'But the people on the train?'

'Screw them. Probably all English, anyway.'

Daniel was trying to pull his friend away from the suspect mini-bus, but Rageh would not go. Instead, he rushed to the driver's side door and yanked it open. Still the man did not change his expression or attitude. Rageh grabbed him by his lapels and yanked him out of the vehicle, down onto the road, stopping the flow of cars in the opposite direction. Against his better judgement, Daniel was there, too, pulling on the man. Both friends realised that however far they dragged the man across the road and up onto the far pavement, a wire was stretched out with them.

'Hold his arms!' screamed Daniel. 'Stop him pressing his

trigger thing.'

The train got louder, until it was roaring overhead, across the bridge. Still Rageh and Daniel dragged the silent man away, towards a field. The noise of the train filled their heads, and the wire stretched even more, and people were out of their cars, staring in utter disbelief.

The train went by, safely. Rageh and Daniel collapsed to the ground with the man. The noise of the train slowly faded away. The mini-bus exploded in a massive orange fireball, the blast rushing sideways after hitting the underside of the bridge to engulf the nearest cars, smoke everywhere, and the old bridge, all blackened stone, with gravel and railway lines above, collapsed down into the fiery bomb crater.


Lily directed Anthony through Newbury town centre, as best as she could remember from her one and only visit, and they were lucky to hit upon the locality of her brother's house without getting very lost.

'I bet you're excited, Lily,' said Maria, smiling.

Lily beamed from ear to ear. She connected hands with Maria. Then she became a little pensive at the thought of trying to convince Ari of the craziness of what was taking place.

'This lane, Anthony. Take this lane, please.'

The sun was making a cornfield look spectacularly beautiful. There were horses to the other side of the lane.

'Is your brother as sultry as you?' asked Maria.

'Hey,' objected Bodie, grinning. 'I'm sat just here, you know.'

Maria smiled, and looked about her. 'It's lovely around here.'

Professor Siddiq was squinting against the sun. 'What's that I can see?'

'What's what?' asked Anthony.

Professor Siddiq pointed. 'There.'

A small black shape was hovering over the cornfield, and it was not a UFO. Anthony slammed on the brakes.

It was Bodie who managed to identify the object. 'Jesus, it's a drone. They've got drones after us now. Anthony, what do we do?'

Lily burst out crying, terrified that she was not to see her brother, after all. It was difficult to turn around the big Porsche on the narrow lane. They would have to go on to the house first.

'Shall we shoot it?' asked Professor Siddiq.

'We only have two bullets, Professor,' pointed out Bodie.

They all watched the drone, as it wobbled left and right, and then it moved away, and vanished beyond a line of trees.

'All right,' said Anthony. 'We're committed now. On to that house.'

He put the Porsche into gear, gunned it and took them to the house, stopping in a cloud of dust. Lily jumped out first, followed by Bodie, his gun drawn.

All was quiet. For some reason, Bodie saw Dan in his mind's eye, maybe because his friend used to deliver things for a living, and this house looked empty. Then the evil-looking drone came around the corner of the house. Everyone froze. Bodie was reluctant to waste his last two bullets, but he tried to take aim at the oscillating object.

'No! No!' came a voice, and then they were joined by Aaron Ford, controlling his drone with the handset. 'Don't shoot it, man! Hey, come on.'

They were all shocked; they were faced by a young guy, in civilian clothes and blue baseball cap, but his voice was American, so there was trepidation because of that.

'Bring the thing down,' ordered Bodie.

'Okay. Chill out.'

Aaron landed the drone with great skill - if any of the others had tried that, it would have dropped like a stone and shattered.

'Who are you people?' asked Aaron. 'What's with the gun?'

Bodie waved the gun. 'Listen, chief. The gun means you say who you are first. Do you get that?'

'My name's Aaron Ford.'

Bodie acted satisfied with that. 'It's Aaron Ford, everyone.'

Lily stepped forward. 'Where's my brother? Where's Ari?'

'You're Ari's sister? You must be Lily? He's talked about you. I'm a friend of Ari's. They invited me to stay for a few days. But they're not here. I've just been hanging out, waiting.'

Anthony went across and discovered that the front door was locked. He rang the doorbell. 'Lily, does your brother drive?'

'Yes. An Audi. And Sarah has a car, too.'

Anthony moved over to Aaron and frisked him. 'He seems genuine,' he said to the others.

Professor Siddiq was inspecting the black drone, with its eight tiny little propellers, and the camera in its belly. Aaron was so proud of it, that he ignored the guy with the gun, and moved over to wax lyrical about his toy.

Bodie put his gun away, satisfied that the American was for real. He turned his attention to the house - jeez, he had just dumped a girl with rich relatives. Lily was looking through the window. Then she took out her cell and tried to ring Ari, but to no avail.

'Lily?' asked Bodie. 'Is this place like your family home in Surabaya?'

Lily's eyes went wide. '*Nooo.*'

'So..?' asked Anthony, looking mainly at Bodie, encouraging him to speak with Lily.

Bodie walked over to the girl. 'Lily, baby. Your brother's not here. You know we can't wait around.'

'I know, Bodie. I understand. It's okay.'

Maria joined them and hugged Lily. Bodie turned to Anthony.

'Do we need anything from here?' asked Anthony. 'Do you think we should break in?'

Bodie shook his head. He looked at the drone. 'Aaron, mate? Is that your hobby, or something?'

'That's right.'

Bodie wanted rid of the stranger. 'Well, what are you doing now? Waiting here for Ari to show up?'

Lily liked the look of the cool American. There was a twinkle in his eye. 'Bodie,' she said. 'He can come with us.'

'Where to?' asked Aaron.

Bodie grinned at Anthony, who shrugged his shoulders.

'Lily,' said Bodie. 'Take Aaron aside and give him the talk.'

You know... the talk.'

While Lily was telling Aaron about the imminent end of human civilisation, the others sat around in the sunshine.

'How are we doing for time, Professor?' asked Anthony.

'Let's just say, I feel late.'

Anthony grimaced. Lily soon rejoined them.

'How did that go?' Bodie asked her.

'He's feeling a little unwell, all of a sudden. But I think he believed me.'

It was a bit cramped in the back of the Porsche, but Bodie was more than happy to be pressed up against Maria. Lily talked with Aaron, to stop him from dwelling on things; he told her about his English travels, and asked her all about Indonesia. He questioned her about the island of Bali, but she hadn't actually been there. They seemed to hit it off straight away. Bodie was fine with that, but Professor Siddiq was a bit put out. With a little huff, he decided to sink down in the front seat and try to sleep.

Anthony was still driving, going south on the A34, loving the Porsche Cayenne, loving that he had taken the brand name away from that psychotic people smuggler, Henry, in Sheffield. What a world away that now felt. Now he was chasing the biggest story of his career, and there would probably be nobody to report it to. For a brief moment, he allowed himself to think again about Anne-Marie, back in Woodseats, with her child. He quickly shook her from his mind. He put his fist over his shoulder and Bodie connected with it. 'How's everyone, back there?'

'Maria's fallen asleep, and Lily is moving to America.'

Lily giggled and slapped his leg.

Aaron looked out the window and watched the English countryside go by. He was thinking about his family, back in Missouri, and then about what Lily had told him. It seemed feasible; he had experienced the plague of flies, the deaths of his two work colleagues, he had seen the non-stop horror of terrorism all over the news. But, of course, this crazy crew could be way off the mark. He was still scared, but okay to go along for the ride - his wanderlust was being satisfied, and he had met this gorgeous Indonesian girl.

Professor Siddiq found that he could not sleep in a moving car, so sat up. 'Where are we?' he asked Anthony.

'We're just north of Winchester. I think that's where we join the M3 for the final run into Southampton.'

Aaron leant forward towards Professor Siddiq. 'Professor, I'm still a little unclear about where Iowa and the other two places come into all this.'

Professor Siddiq half turned. 'I assume, when world governments are planning to kill ninety-nine per cent of the population, that things don't go according to plan. To give you an example, I think the British government recently paid a couple of billion pounds for new fighter jets that can't fly in the rain. Politicians are morons. So, with something this massive, there are bound to be little accidents. Some of this toxin managed to escape, and where it happened to come down was: Iowa, Berkshire and Jakarta, by pure bad luck. That's just my theory, Aaron, for what it's worth.'

'Thank you, Professor.'

Anthony and Professor Siddiq both looked up at the sky, which had suddenly, and frighteningly, gone dark.

'That ain't good,' said Anthony. 'Do you remember what happened at Wembley stadium?'

'Should we stop, do you think?'

'Well, we need gas, anyway. And there's a petrol station coming up. We can get inside there if the storm comes on.'

Anthony pulled onto the petrol station forecourt, as the day had almost turned to night. 'You should wake Maria up,' he told Bodie.

'Are we having a storm?' asked Lily.

'Hopefully nothing more than that,' replied Professor Siddiq. 'Let's all go into the shop, while Anthony fills the tank.'

They got out of the Porsche and felt the wind trying to knock them off their feet. Everyone went into the shop, while Anthony battled at the pump to fill the car. The cashier was a young Asian man, looking worryingly out at the sky. He did actually check out Lily, but then the terrifying sky took his attention. Aaron and Lily checked along the shelves of English confectionery, something which never failed to fascinate.

Anthony finished brimming the Porsche's petrol tank and replaced the cap, and put the hose back on the pump. Then he wanted to get into the shop, but the wind was keeping him pinned to the spot. Above him, the station canopy started to lift. The screeching noise was suddenly tremendous, like a train passing right by his head. Anthony looked up, expecting to see a tornado pass by, but, instead, he saw that the sky was in turmoil, like a vortex. Trees flew by at a vast pace. The noise was added to, and Anthony turned his face fractionally to see a moderately sized passenger aircraft struggling to make any headway. He could not believe how it was staying up, its engines must have been at full throttle. As he watched in horror, the plane was lifted to starboard, and then it was over on its back. Anthony was flashed back to his childhood near Manchester airport, with all that fear about terrorists spraying poison from light aircraft, but he also realised that he had dreamed about what he was currently seeing - it was the strongest event of deja-vu that he had ever felt in his life.

The plane had stalled, upside down, and it was about to come down. Terrified, Anthony managed to move his feet, running in treacle to the shop, where Bodie pulled him through the door.

The aircraft came down right beside the petrol station, with parts of the starboard wings crashing into the building. Anthony landed on Bodie. Professor Siddiq threw himself on top of Maria to protect her, just as the roof came in with terrible noise and dust, and then total blackness.

Lily and Aaron had been knocked into the store room, and were lying in the chaos of masonry and sparking electrical wiring, and with boxes of crisps and nuts exploded all across them. Lily cleared her eyes, deciding quickly that she was unhurt. But then she felt wetness on both legs, and she could smell fuel. She realised that she could just about see through the debris because of fires, close by. Fear grabbed her.

'Aaron?' she called.

'Here,' he answered, weakly.

Lily could see him in a small pocket of brickwork and shelving. He was bleeding heavily from the left side of his head. Lily forced herself to move. 'Aaron, stay still, I'm coming to you.'

Lily needed to crawl through to where Aaron was. But it was a tight space, like pot-holing, and the concrete ceiling seemed less than safe. Nevertheless, she moved onwards, only to have Professor Siddiq grab her ankles.

'Lily, no,' warned the Professor, his voice desperate. 'That's coming down.'

'No, Salman. I must. Let go! Let go, please.'

Lily gave a little kick out to free her legs, and then began squirming through the terrifyingly tight space. Professor Siddiq watched with bated breath, praying for the ceiling to hold, but then she was through, and kneeling beside Aaron, tearing at a staff room towel to wrap around Aaron's wound.

There was nothing for it, but for Professor Siddiq to go through, as well. Feeling his back scraping the concrete, a wave of awful claustrophobia engulfing him, he got himself across, and rolled away in total relief. Then he rooted around in the small room, actually finding a decent First Aid kit. Working together with Lily, they managed to bandage up Aaron's head; clearly he was still bleeding, but it was no longer a torrent.

The air was getting bad with acrid smoke. Fire flickered through the shell of the back wall of the building. Professor Siddiq hated to admit it, but they had to take Aaron back the way they had come.

'Lily, we have to get him out of here.'

'Yes.'

They started to drag the groaning Aaron towards the space.

Professor Siddiq took his life in his hands and pushed himself back under the concrete slab. He was so relieved to squirt back out the other side, but the worst was the follow. Lily was pushing Aaron as hard as she could. Professor Siddiq, hearing Bodie and Anthony behind him, had to stretch under, and pull with all his might. Gradually, Aaron's body was dragged out. Professor Siddiq handed the American over to the others; his only thought then was to get Lily out.

The ceiling creaked. Lily was getting out, or Lily was going to be crushed, or Lily was being trapped to burn to death. 'Now, Lily.'

Lily simply offered up the prayer, 'Bismillah,' and crawled forward into the space. It moved above her, she cried out, she scrambled in a panic, her beloved Salman had her by the wrists and she was yanked through. She found herself on Professor Siddiq's lap, her face cushioned in his gentle hands.

The roof did not cave in.

'You see?' said Professor Siddiq, trying to use humour to calm her raging blood pressure. 'Safe as houses.'

Anthony and Bodie were shouting for them to get out. Professor Siddiq and Lily scrambled over the mess that had once been the petrol station. Flame roared in the background, but the storm had passed. The scene was one of utter devastation, in a calm setting, and yet the Porsche Cayenne sat there, wet, but completely undamaged in any way. Bodie and Anthony were loading up Aaron. Maria, filthy but unhurt, rushed to Lily.

Everyone was aboard, and Anthony drove them on, down the slick highway, currently devoid of vehicles. Apart from the dirt and the blood, it was as if nothing had happened at all.

# 24

Fifty-six-year-old, sports retail tycoon, Anderson John Caine, with an estimated fortune of £4.4 billion, had recently bought the biggest mansion in the Edgbaston area of Birmingham. He was wondering whether to remove the previous owner's tree from the conservatory, while talking on his cell to his CEO, Ashley Snelson. Unfortunately, the never-ending rain, drumming on the glass roof, made it impossible to hear, so he began drifting from one marble-floored room to the next, considering how he could "bling" the property even more.

'What's with all this rain, Ashley? My garden landscapers are having a terrible time of it.'

Caine still carried a slight South African lilt to his accent, having only moved to the UK at fourteen years of age. One of his wilder business stories revolved around his great-grandfather fighting for the Boers against the tyrannical British.

In the foyer, he gave consideration to his two new, platinum-plated baby elephants, which stood either side of the massive studded front door. Then, through onto the Welsh slate of his kitchen/diner, which had its own conservatory attached, containing an original juke box and his pinball machine. He let Snelson waffle on, down the cell, about sales figures, etc, etc, while thinking about whether he needed some artwork in there. Through the other side of the kitchen, there was an artists' studio, where his thirty-year-old wife, Hannah, occasionally painted with oils, and then into his sixteen-seat home cinema, with photos of all the oldies on the wall: Humphrey Bogart, James Cagney et al.

Caine moved along a corridor, which Hannah had decorated with gold wallpaper, and with busts of people like Julius Caesar and Che Guevara (why, he had not asked). It led to his snooker room, which had dark-panelled walls and an antique green light canopy over the table. Through the rain-streaked windows he had a view of his triple garage, which held his black Ferrari 360, his silver Porsche 911, and his collection of bright red 1930's *Indian* motorcycles. He decided that he must speak with his US contact and try to get himself another one of those, whatever the cost.

He could just about make out his team of landscapers, far off in the grounds. He wanted the rain to stop so he could go out and confer with them.

'Ashley, let's talk about the work practices in the warehouses.' He went through into one of the lounges, which was so big that it could have accommodated four regular-sized living areas, with televisions. Near to the French windows, stood his wife's Grand piano. 'Specifically, Ashley, you know how we monitor the staff for every second that they are on duty? Well, I think they take too many toilet breaks. Could we make the staff wear diapers?' There was a long pause, the other end. 'Ashley? Ashley, are you still there? I was joking.' He laughed loudly.

Caine moved through to his office, which resembled the Oval office of the White House. The rain lashed the windows one last time and then went quiet. He sat at his desk, looking at his recent birthday present: a bronze bust of his wife's perfect derriere. He ran his eyes over the art on the walls. Also, in pride of place, was a framed document from a well-known High Street bank, dated October 1997, refusing him a personal loan for just £2000. He had come an awful long way since then. He had hated the rich, back then. Now, he hated the poor, and had nothing but utter contempt for the people who worked as virtual slaves for him.

'Ashley? No, seriously, you know how we monitor their time and motion? Well, can we not film them on CCTV while on the shop floor, and if they discuss anything that's not to do with work, we sack them? Ashley? Ashley, no, really serious this time.'

Ashley Snelson was talking to his boss, while a passenger in one of the firm's helicopters, heading towards the mansion.

Rain streaked the front canopy, but the pilot had just assured him that the squall had just passed, and they would have no trouble landing on the concrete helipad.

'Mr Caine, sir. We are approaching now, sir. I will hang up now, and we shall cover that issue, once I get there. Okay, sir? Yes, I will make sure to come around the back because of the mud. Hanging up now, sir.'

With that, he turned off his cell, put it in his jacket pocket, said a swear word, and tried to enjoy the ride.

He saw the big, white monstrosity of a building, as they came down through grey cloud. He hated Anderson Caine. Hated him with a vengeance. But the pay was very good; Caine paid well for the people who saved him more money with efficient work practices imposed on the bottom feeder scum of the warehouses and stores.

The pilot was gently bringing the helicopter in to land. Snelson watched through the port-side window. Suddenly, inexplicably, the ten-bedroom, £10 million property disappeared downwards. It was the craziest thing Snelson had ever seen in his life; so much so that he felt his eyes were playing tricks on him. The pilot was gabbling wildly into his ear, equally astonished. Instead of landing, the helicopter began to hover, so the two men could survey the unbelievable scene. All that remained was a massive black hole in the ground; a massive, horrible black hole. The mansion, together with Anderson Caine, had sunk into a giant sink hole, without trace - house, garages, driveway, pool house, and parts of the lawns and tennis courts, gone.

In 2016, Winchester was named as the best place to live in England.

The six occupants of the Porsche Cayenne loved the city on first sight, following the boring road that had been the never-ending A34. They parked in the first shopping area that they came across, and Anthony stepped out, to be able to look around. He brushed dust from his hair. Luckily, right there in front of him, stood a small medical walk-in clinic.

Anthony and Bodie took an arm each of Aaron, and frogmarched the injured American towards the clinic.

'I've been here before,' said Aaron, looking around, with glassy eyes.

Bodie looked at Anthony. 'The boy's delirious.'

Patients, sitting in the waiting area, stared at them (they must have looked a sight), and a nurse tried to challenge them, but they kept moving until they stumbled into a doctor. At gunpoint, they made the elderly male physician deal with Aaron's head wounds.

'What film is this a scene from?' asked Anthony.

Bodie gave it some thought. '*Heat.*'

'That's right, *Heat*, where Robert De Niro makes the doctor work on Tom Sizemore.'

The doctor looked up from his work on Aaron's head, and said, in a deadpan tone, 'It was Val Kilmer, actually.'

They stepped out of the medical centre into the sunshine. There was the smell of freshly baked bread in the air, from a nearby bakery, which was comforting. There were hanging baskets of pretty flowers everywhere. Definitely a nice part of the world.

Aaron was more lucid, by then, able to walk unaided. Anthony looked about him, glad that the police were clearly too busy with the aftermath of the tornado to respond to their trifling gun offence in the medical centre. Aaron was settled happily between the two girls, who both started to mother him, and they got away from that part of town.

Before they joined the M3, Anthony pulled over in a lay-by, so that everyone could have something to eat, and they could check that they were all okay, and ready for the big push into Southampton.

'It could get hairy down there,' said Anthony. 'Everyone stick together. When we see the chance, we'll use the guns to gain access... ferry-side, if that's how it's described.'

'Can I make a suggestion?' asked Bodie. 'If someone gets hurt from now on, we leave them behind. We can't be carrying bodies on to ferries.'

Professor Siddiq nodded. 'That sounds fair and correct.'

Bodie grinned. 'As Dan would have said, "harsh, harsh but fair".'

Professor Siddiq then got out of the car, to go behind a tree to relieve himself. On returning, he had Lily taking him into an embrace.

'Salman, you were so brave, back there.'

'Behind the tree?'

'No, at the plane crash.'

'Absolute nonsense, my dear. You were the brave one. Extraordinarily brave to do what you did. I'm very proud of you.'

Lily sniffled against his shoulder. They both giggled. He had a thought, which made him laugh.

'What is it?'

'I just had a vision of us with those donkeys, back in Wrangle village. Bizarre to think of that, I suppose.'

'No, it's not. It was a lovely time there. I was so nervous beside you. I imagined you were my husband and that was our garden.'

Professor Siddiq was greatly touched to hear that. Shocked, but also touched. 'You sweet, sweet girl.'

Bodie called to them. It was time to go. Time for their end game to start.

Anthony continued to do the driving; it was his Porsche, after all. Professor Siddiq managed to drop off to sleep, in the front seat. Lily had found some *Wet Wipes* in a seat pocket and started to gently clean the parts of Aaron's face not done by the doctor. Bodie took some from her and tried to do the same to Maria, who screamed with laughter, fending him off. He leant in, and whispered, 'But I want to kiss a clean part of your neck.'

'Behave yourself, you naughty boy.'

'You're so cute.'

'I know.'

'Remember when we used to talk about babies?'

'Oh, my, yes. You and your silly name choices.'

'I still don't think there's anything wrong with Cody Bodie.'

'Well, it would have been Cody Cowfield-Bodie.'

Lily interjected. 'Oh, that's so much better.'

'Do you mind?' asked Bodie, pretending to be offended. 'So, Maria, still reckon on keeping your surname, do you? Anyway...' He watched to see that Lily was talking with Aaron, before saying to Maria, 'Whatever happens from now on, stay at my side. I go through with you, or I don't go through at all.'

Maria smiled and rested her head on his shoulder.

Anthony drove on at a steady seventy mph. He checked his cell: dead. He checked the car's radio: dead. They were clearly going into a technology black-out area.

'So, you're loving your new car, cousin?' asked Bodie.

'Too right. When we come out from all this, I'll be getting me one of these.'

'I'm not that keen on the shape, personally. I tell you what, the third next big thing that passes us, I'll get one of those.'

Anthony checked his mirror. 'You're on.'

They watched a Nissan Note overtake them. Then, after a gap, an old BMW 5 series. After that, there came a big Mitsubishi Land Cruiser.

'There's the first big thing,' said Anthony.

Next, a white van passed.

'I suppose that's big,' said Anthony. 'Number two.'

Finally, after a Mini Cooper, a coach passed them. Anthony laughed raucously.

A few minutes later, with Bodie watching the traffic, and the people going about their normal lives, a Mercedes 4x4 came slowly past. Bodie looked at it admiringly, and casually at the people inside. Bodie glanced at the passenger, and the passenger glanced at Bodie. The man's face gradually comprehended that he knew Bodie. The passenger in the

Mercedes was the American Agent, Harrison, from Old Leake.

'We've got trouble,' said Bodie.

Bodie watched as Harrison held a frantic conversation with his driving colleague, and then the Mercedes started slamming into the side of the Porsche. Anthony realised what was happening and fought back by turning his steering wheel violently to the right. Professor Siddiq had woken into another drama, and the others in the back were highly concerned.

On went the battering, screeching and thudding, the Mercedes gradually forcing the Porsche over until they came to a juddering, entangled halt on the hard shoulder, with other vehicles avoiding the "accident". Harrison climbed out, one arm still in a sling, a gun in his free hand. Anthony had no chance to react, he was faced with the barrel of the gun through the side window, and the other agent, the driver, was there quickly, ordering everyone out of the back.

Bodie stepped down. Harrison turned his gaze to Bodie, and the gun followed. He took deliberate aim at Bodie's head.

'I'm sorry about this,' said Harrison.

Before Harrison could execute Bodie, Lily stepped into view, raised one of the taser weapons, aimed at Harrison's chest and fired. The two prongs hit the American in the throat, delivering 50,000 volts, shaking him, making him silently scream and then drop to the ground.

Bodie leapt forward, took Harrison's weapon, ready to kill the other man. But Harrison's partner had, surprisingly, holstered his weapon and was listening to information coming through his earpiece. Anthony went over to the man, spoke to him, and Bodie watched, fascinated, as a friendly handshake took place.

'It's over, Bodie,' said Anthony. 'The agents have been called off.'

The man offered a handshake to Bodie, which was accepted. 'I'm Bill.'

'Bodie. Nice to meet you.'

'Clearly they feel we no longer pose a threat to their plans,' said Anthony.

Bodie turned back to a prostrate Harrison, who had Lily and Maria tending to him. Harrison was ghostly pale, and, with his arm in a sling, he looked quite comical.

'Miss, did you just taser me?' Harrison asked Lily.

'Yes, I did. I'm sorry about that.'


Professor Siddiq sat with Harrison and Bill on the grassy bank, at the side of the motorway. Bodie stood with Anthony, watching on.

'Bodie, mate, remember back in Sheffield, we didn't expect all this.'

'No, it has been tougher.'

'The Professor gives a good End of the World speech.'

'True.'

A breakdown truck, from a major recovery company, slowed alongside them, the driver looking at them through his open window.

'Drive on,' called Anthony, waving. 'We're *The Sweeney*, son, and everyone here's getting nicked.'

The driver gave Anthony a funny look, before speeding away into traffic. Bodie laughed.

Bill began to rock backwards and forwards, with his head in his hands.

'The Prof has got to a good part,' pointed out Bodie.

Bill stood up and started to wander about like a tranquilised rhino. When he went near to the traffic flow, Harrison got up to bring him back, and sit him down.

'Do you think they'll join us?' asked Bodie.

'Why shouldn't they? They can see what's going on for themselves. Bodie, mate, if we come through this, and the worst actually happens, I can't imagine ever going north again.'

'No, me neither. I hear Brighton is nice.'

'Think smaller. A small town.'

'Why?'

'Fewer corpses to deal with.'

'Oh, I see.'

The meeting came to an end. Harrison stood up, dusted himself down and came over to them, rubbing the two puncture holes in his neck. 'Feisty girl you've got there. Well, boys, it's a lot to take in.'

'It is that,' said Bodie.

They examined the damage to the vehicles, deciding that it was not too serious.

'Where's the hippy fellow?' asked Harrison.

'He didn't make it,' answered Bodie.

'Damn. I'm sorry to hear that.'

'What about your colleague, from Old Leake?'

'She's Stateside now. Doing okay, last I heard.' He realised what he was saying. 'Or, maybe, not doing so okay, as it turns out. Come on, we've got a ferry to catch.'

Anthony followed the Mercedes along the motorway.

'We're experiencing it all on this trip, aren't we, Professor?'

'Yes, we certainly are. I'm glad the American agents are on our side now.'

'So am I. Two nice guys, as well. Apart from damaging my Porsche like that.'

'So, we go into the ferry port with them?'

'Looks like it. See, I told you it would work out.' He looked in his mirror. 'All right in the back?'

'All right in the back,' everyone replied, except for the quiet Aaron.

'It's gravy now. Into the docks, onto the ferry, Bob's your uncle. A few hours. All right, Aaron?'

'All right in the back,' answered Aaron, causing them all to laugh.

# 25

Kamikaze attacks were taking place all around the world, either genuinely planned or copycat events; from Baghdad to Copenhagen, from Auckland to Munich.

His full name was Henry John Rossiter, originally from Birmingham, with a background in road haulage, door staff management, extortion and, finally, people smuggling. He had a long-term partner and six-year-old child, at their large barn conversion in Buxton, Derbyshire. To all intensive purposes he was an upstanding businessman. He had been, briefly, upset to discover that a reporter had infiltrated his pan-European smuggling operation, but held no grudge against the young man involved, who was only trying to make his way in the world, just like he was.

Henry was standing on a walkway over a tram line, at one of the Southampton ferry terminals, having arrived there that morning. He didn't believe all the nonsense that foolish people were spouting, about a conspiracy, and he had no desire to flee the mainland. He was there solely because he revelled in other people's misery; it was his thing, his fetish. His camera was with him, and he was snapping away at the throngs of desperate refugees below, as they were pushed back by British Transport Police, and who fought amongst themselves, in their hopeless despair. His face was impassive, but he was grinning inside; it was like the Wimbledon final to him, like the British Grand Prix. The people moved like shoals of fish escaping sharks, and some were getting trampled. *Marvellous.*

From his elevated position, Henry saw the man appear on the roof of the terminal building. He photographed him all the way across, caught the man as he offered up a prayer, and snapped him all the way down, as he dive-bombed the heaving mass of people below. Henry spread his arms and raised his eyes in his own prayer - what a scoop! *Thank you, God.*

Ari and Sarah were caught up in the mob, after trying for hours to find a policeman willing to help them talk to a senior officer. The police had not been briefed properly, and, as a result, were unclear as to why the port was being stormed. The order had come to push the people back. Ari and Sarah were trying to hold on to one another. The crush was getting desperate. Sarah feared that her fingers would slip from Ari's. Ironically, the body falling into the crowd, very close to them, however disgusting, did create a breathing space, allowing Ari to tuck Sarah against his body and push them away to relative safety. They moved to the far side of a concrete pillar, then embraced as strongly as they had ever done before.

Still quite far from Southampton, the traffic on the motorway came to a standstill. Anthony stayed behind the Mercedes - for the first time he entertained thoughts of not making it to safety in time.

They waited, and waited. Eventually, Harrison and Bill stood from the Mercedes, as other people were doing, from their own vehicles.

'A bit of a delay,' Anthony said, over his shoulder. 'Stretch your legs, you guys.'

Half a mile away, to the left of the motorway, a junior cricket match was taking place, despite the inclement weather. Several people moved to the barrier to look out over it.

'Thank God the plane didn't come down over there,' said Maria. 'They look sweet in their white clothes.'

'The outfield must be soaking,' said Bodie. 'Oh, good shot! Lily, that was a sweep shot.'

Lily rolled her eyes. 'Yeah, like you know anything about cricket.'

A short delivery was hooked over the boundary rope and plopped into a river at the side of the field. The spectators on the motorway applauded. Bodie held Maria from behind, as they watched, and, even though Lily was nearby, Maria didn't object.

Actually, Lily was busy talking to Aaron. She was concentrating hard as he took her through the basics of baseball.

'You don't have to support the *Royals*,' he said. 'I don't

mind.'

'Well, who can I support, then?'

'Anyone but the *New York Yankees*. Name a city in the States that you want to visit, and I'll tell you their team.'

'I don't want to visit America.'

Aaron was a bit taken aback. 'Do you not?'

'But, let me think. How about San Francisco? I am Lily Fransisca, after all.'

'The *San Francisco Giants*.'

'Yes, yes, they're now my team.'

Lily skipped over to Professor Siddiq, dipping into his bag of Ready Salted crisps. 'Salman, I'm now a *San Francisco Giants* fan.'

'Are you really? I'm pleased for you.'

There came a sudden loud noise. Everyone looked to the sky, fearing another tornado, but the sky was clear. The rumbling continued.

'Earthquake?' asked Bodie. 'Surely not.'

'It's not an earthquake,' said Lily.

What it was, was the river; a huge torrent of water went flooding down, alongside the motorway, dirty brown, carrying tree stumps and a small car. Everyone watched in shock as it rushed by; then, as it reached a bend in the river, it burst its banks, sending millions of gallons of floodwater across the cricket field. The boys didn't stand a chance, swept away in a tsunami of mud and debris, all the way down into a neighbouring field.

Even in the middle of their own disaster, dozens of members of the public clambered over the guard rail and hurried over the fields to help. Maria had turned away and buried her face in Bodie's chest, while Lily had done the same with Professor Siddiq.

'Should we go and help?' asked Aaron.

'No, point,' answered Anthony, rubbing his shoulder.

Anthony pulled on his beard and marched back and forth, staring at the traffic that blocked his way. Then he remembered: Aaron's drone. 'Aaron. That drone of yours. If we got off the motorway, could you use it to find us a route across country?'

'Sure, I guess.'

Bodie stared at his cousin, but then realised it was not such a bad idea. In normal life, nobody would attempt to try to get anywhere off the side of a motorway - but it was no longer normal life. Anthony quickly looked up and down the hard shoulder, looking for a ramp where the traffic police park their vehicles, a way through the barriers, and he spotted exactly that.

'We go through that gap. Then Aaron is our eyes through the fields, until we find a way into Southampton. Okay?' Everyone nodded. 'I'll go tell the Americans. Pile in.'

Harrison and Bill listened, and were keen on the plan. Anthony ran back and got the Porsche moving; he was on point. They drove down the hard shoulder, went up the ramp, and were then faced with a fairly steep drop. Anthony was committed, taking them over the edge. All passengers pressed their hands on the ceiling; it was that extreme, like a ride at an amusement park. The Porsche slithered, rocked, wheel-spun, but inched down towards a farmer's field. Anthony wiped out a wooden fence, before braking, and watching Bill bringing down the Mercedes.

Aaron went to the boot, brought out his drone and the controller. Everyone watched with growing excitement as he set it up, all the little propellers whizzing around, and it slowly lifted off. Professor Siddiq got in the back, allowing Aaron up front, alongside Anthony, and they were off across the field. The little screen showed the farmer's fields, then the snake of stalled traffic, up on the motorway, before Aaron spotted an old stone bridge, over the swollen river.

'Tell me I'm a genius,' said Anthony.

Aaron declined to do that, concentrating on the screen. The two cars bumped along, sometimes taking a farm track, sometimes staying to the fields, destroying crops as they went. Aaron was enjoying his vacation again, despite having a plane fall on his head. He was with amazing people, doing an amazing thing, and he was loving it.

'Use the bridge, Anthony,' he said. 'Then go left on the road, yes, now turn right and head through this field.'

It was slow going, but anything was better than sitting on the motorway. They passed through small hamlets, always heading south. On the roads they used, briefly, they encountered heavy traffic, but they were soon back going cross-country. At one stage, they traversed a golf course, much to the rage of several golfers. Then, before they knew it, they were bursting through trees and out onto a normal street, and the drone lowered down to show them a road sign, which pointed the way to the university.

Anthony checked an A-to-Z map, from the driver's door

pocket. 'University of Southampton. No doubt a top institution. That way will do us fine.'

Bodie and Lily exchanged grins at the mention of another university. Aaron got out to collect his drone, and then Anthony led the two cars into the heart of Southampton.

Professor Siddiq heard Lily's stomach rumble, and they both laughed. 'Are you hungry, dear?'

'A little. What I wouldn't give for some *Ayam Pop* right now.'

He laughed. 'That sounds fun. What is it?'

'It's fried chicken.'

'Oh, wow, get me some, too.'

Their small convoy was approaching what looked like Armageddon; cars abandoned everywhere, army helicopters circling, people moping around in a zombie-like state. Anthony drove them slowly in further. There seemed to be tear gas drifting away on the wind. Anthony's heart sank again. Strangely, he imagined himself shaving off his beard, then sitting down on a patch of grass somewhere, looking at the sky, waiting for whatever was to happen, to go ahead and happen.

Bill was sounding his horn, so Anthony stopped. Their only real hope lay with the Americans, so they all climbed out of the Porsche and went to stay close to Harrison and Bill.

'We're going to talk with those English police officers, over there,' said Harrison.

Lily needed a hug, so moved into the willing arms of Professor Siddiq.

'Are you all right?' he asked.

'I'm thinking about my parents. About the day I heard that I'd been accepted by the university. I don't regret coming to England. If this had to happen, then I'm with the nicest of people. Especially you, Salman.'

Harrison and Bill returned to them, brushing past the aimless wanderings of members of the public. Everyone looked at Harrison with trepidation.

'All the ferries have left,' he reported. 'And to quote that English police inspector, "all the Yankees have skedaddled."'

'*Mr Tony!?*'

'What now?' asked Maria.

'*Mr Tony!?*'

'What do we do?' asked Lily.

'*Hey, Mr Tony!?*'

The overriding thought was: that there was nothing more to be done. The horrifying scenario began to sink in. One by one, they realised that they were being heckled from above, and all their faces turned.

'Hey, Mr Tony, say cheese.'

Henry Rossiter was still on his walkway, and aiming his camera at them.

'What the hell is this now?' asked Harrison.

Anthony recognised Henry from Sheffield. Even at the lowest point ever in his life, he was still shocked and surprised.

'You left us suddenly, Mr Tony. I was very disappointed. Who are your friends? I tell you, every one of you are extremely photogenic.'

Anthony really did not know what to do. It was like life was mocking him. He wanted to climb the walkway and beat the nasty man to a pulp. But what was the point?

Bodie had realised who the man was, and was equally surprised. He tugged at Anthony's arm, indicated for them all to leave; to leave that place and go anywhere. Anywhere at all.

'Let's get out of here,' said Anthony.

'Oh, no you don't,' called Henry. He let his camera dangle down onto his chest, and pulled a hand gun from under his sweater. He aimed at Anthony and fired. The bullet ricocheted off the pavement, causing people to scatter in panic. Bodie and Professor Siddiq protected the girls. Anthony stood his ground, livid with people, and with the world in general. He drew his gun, knowing it was empty, and aimed at Henry. Henry fired twice more, proving inaccurate in his own craziness.

Harrison brought out his gun quicker than Bill. He aimed at the easy target, just above him, and put a bullet squarely through Henry's forehead, sending a fine spray of red mist outwards to the rear. Henry simply looked stunned for a fraction of a second, before tumbling backwards into the crowds.

# 26

Lily and Maria climbed into the back of the Porsche, for their own safety. The men tried to decide what to do next.

'We might as well go eat,' suggested Bill.

'A nice steak and kidney pudding?' asked Bodie.

'Hell, no. Chicken, somewhere.'

'*KFC*?' suggested Professor Siddiq. 'There you are, Lily. *KFC* for you.'

'It's not the same as *Ayam Pop*,' said Lily. 'But I want some, anyway.'

Anthony spread his arms wide. 'Let's go eat, then. It's as good as anything else we could do.'

They returned to their separate vehicles, intending to head away from the docks, and find some normal civilisation, within the city. As Anthony began to make the Porsche turn in a circle, Lily was suddenly out of her door, running away.

'Ari!' screamed Lily. 'Ari!'

At the last second, Lily had spotted her brother and his wife. She ran to him and, as Ari realised with delight, he opened his arms to receive her, and they hugged fiercely. All their emotions flooded out, and they were in tears. Lily tried to express her relief at finding him, her face wet from the crying, and then she hugged Sarah. Professor Siddiq had rushed after her, then stood there, heartened to see the family reconciliation.

They drove onto a retail park. Lily was riding in the Mercedes, catching up with her brother and sister-in-law. It had not been difficult to persuade them to come away from the ferry terminal.

Unfortunately, there was no *KFC*, but there was a branch of the restaurant chain that Bodie worked for.

'I wonder if I'll get my staff discount,' joked Bodie.

They took two booths, next to each other, ordering almost everything on the menu.

'Let's go out with a big greedy blow-out,' said Anthony, laughing.

They had pitchers of beer, and milkshakes for Lily and Professor Siddiq. The televisions were on, but were blank - clearly the whole of Southampton was blacked out, as far as the media was concerned. The friendly waitress served them, as she would any other big party, keen on her large tip to come. There were families in the restaurant, lots of balloons, and one rendition of *Happy Birthday*. It was such a normal scene that it seemed impossible to believe what was about to happen.

Plates of large barbequed ribs, and potato skins with soured cream, and golden fries arrived.

Bodie looked over at Lily, who was in the other booth. 'You okay?'

'Yes and no. I'm okay, but it's puzzling to see such competent waiters.'

Bodie made a big surprised O shape with his mouth, then slapped her ponytail. 'You cheeky mare.'

The meal progressed happily. Everyone laughed when Professor Siddiq revealed that he was having his first ever milkshake.

'And your last!' joked Anthony, causing great hilarity.

Bodie clinked glasses with Anthony. 'Anthony.'

'Bodie.'

'Here we are. Is this it, then? We stop now?'

'What do you suggest? We steal a light aircraft?'

'What about a boat? From somewhere along the coast.'

Anthony downed his beer, looking at his cousin across the table. Then he got up and went out to the Porsche, returning with a map, which he spread out over the food, providing much hindrance to Maria's enjoyment of her meal. They scanned down to the south coast, seeing the familiar shape of the Isle of Wight, with Southampton above it, Portsmouth to the east.

'What's all this green area, to the west?' asked Anthony.

'That's the New Forest.'

While Southampton was to the north of the Isle of Wight, across the Solent, the New Forest moved down around it. Anthony traipsed his finger down until he reached the coast, only a short distance across the water. 'Maybe we just need to get somewhere less congested than Southampton docks.'

'A fishing village?' suggested Bodie. 'Hire a fisherman to take us over.'

Harrison had joined the conversation. 'The waters will be heavily guarded.'

'We can but try,' said Anthony. 'During the night.'

Harrison's finger plonked down on the map. 'That place, there.'

Bodie, although reading upside down, said, 'Lymington.'

The race was back on. Bodie rolled up the map, Harrison went back to Bill.

'Check, please!' called Anthony.

The waitress was taken aback. Anthony pulled an apologetic face. The girl rushed to her till station before hurrying back with the bill on a tray.

Everyone began to head out to the cars. Anthony gave the waitress the money for the bill, then placed on a hundred pound tip. She was astonished, speechless with happiness. Anthony realised that he had nothing to say to the girl, so simply smiled, and chased after the others.

Bill took the lead, pulling the Mercedes out at speed. They quickly left the city to the east. It was normal day-to-day life out there; people catching buses, or walking their dogs. There were delivery vans about, and builders working on roofs. They all watched the world go by, as they grasped at their final chance to survive. The houses became larger, with more land around them. Then it really got rural and very beautiful. It was almost possible to forget the nature of their road trip and settle back to enjoy the scenery.

Bill came to a stop, so Anthony did, too. Then they watched the Americans changing a flat tyre, at the left rear. It only took them ten minutes (Harrison not much help with one hand), but it felt longer. Then they set off again.

Maria rooted about in the centre console between the front seats, finding a pack of cards and some *Liquorice Allsorts*. She started passing the sweets around.

'Anthony, do you want a sweet?' she asked.

'I'll pass, thank you.'

Bodie took the pack of cards. 'Come on, Maria, I'll teach you poker.'

She took them back. 'No, you won't. I'll teach you the game I play with my ten-year-old niece. It's called *Go Boom*.'

Anthony laughed over his shoulder. 'Very apt.'

It was simple to learn, seven cards, placing them down by suit or number, until you had gotten rid of all your cards, then you shouted, "Go boom!"

'How long to Lymington, Anthony?' asked Bodie.

'Not sure.'

'Okay, Maria, first to ten. What does the winner get?'

'A kiss.'

'What does the loser get?'

'The same kiss, stupid.'

Bodie won the first game, after they both went down to just

one card, then back up to collecting thirteen again, before he had a run to the finish. 'Go boom!'

The weather was closing in again, as they went through the town of Lyndhurst, turning south, further into the New Forest. But the rain seemed normal, as it hit the windscreen, and there was no great wind. Bill pushed the Mercedes on, with Anthony doing well to stay with him. They passed through one more village, and then the road signs were telling them that they were close to Lymington, and to the Lymington ferry port.

In the Porsche, there were no more card games, or any talking, they just listened to the rain and the sound of the wipers slapping back and forth. Up ahead, Anthony saw Bill's brake lights come on, as the American slowed into Lymington.

They crawled through the town. There was some traffic heading into the area, but it was not insane, like Southampton. Bill leant out of the Mercedes driver's window to ask directions, and then they carried on.

Soon, they drove into position at the small ferry port, behind a line of blurry red brake lights, with the rain sweeping in horizontally off the Solent. Anthony ran forward to briefly speak to Harrison, then got back into the Porsche and shook the rain from his head.

'Seems like the ferry is still in port,' he said. 'We're in the line. Who knows whether we will get on it, though.'

'Where does it take us?' asked Professor Siddiq.

'Yarmouth, on the east side of the island.'

'Are Lily and her family okay?'

'I didn't ask. Why shouldn't they be?'

They waited. It became steamed up in the Porsche.
Everyone was on edge. Then they saw officials in fluorescent
bibs moving about in the downpour, and vehicles started to
slowly creep forward.

'Here we go,' said Anthony.

It was scary, driving into a port with almost zero visibility.
Anthony was staying in line with Bill's blurry lights.

'It's like *Formula One*,' said Bodie. 'In the wet. But a bit
slower.'

The queue curved to the left, and they could estimate that
they were about tenth or twelfth in line. The road surface
moved from concrete to metal.

Professor Siddiq was starting to fret. 'A ferry? In this
weather? I know, I know, we have to go, but it's so unsafe.'

'Keep it together, Professor,' said Anthony. 'This is wild. We
can't even see the ferry.'

The spray was fifteen, twenty feet high. They just stayed
within the white railings and followed the tail lights of the
Mercedes.

'Actually, I'll be glad to be on deck,' said Professor Siddiq.
'Anything's better than this. We're like animals being led into
the slaughterhouse.'

There were two officials, in their orange bibs, now using
fluorescent paddles to wave the cars forward.

'I'm with you on that, Professor,' said Anthony. 'I want to
feel these wheels on the deck of the ferry.'

The cars ahead started to descend towards the ferry, the
officials getting more and more animated, clearly wanting the
ferry gone, and themselves out of the storm. They watched the

Mercedes edge forward, and then its nose dropped down, and it followed the other cars.

'Stop!' Bodie suddenly shouted. 'Something's not right here, Anthony.'

Anthony held his foot on the brake, looking back anxiously at his cousin.

Bodie got out of the Porsche into the weather, despite Maria trying to hold onto him. He edged forward through the driving rain. The officials were no longer anywhere to be seen. He went forward. Surely, even in the squall, he would have expected to see the docking lights of the ferry. He moved carefully along the metal ramp, and looked over the edge, to where Harrison's vehicle had gone. What he saw, lit by arc-lights, horrified him: there was no ferry, whatsoever, but there were red lights under the swirling waterline, with cars sitting half in and half out of the sea, people scrambling for their lives on roofs and bonnets, vehicles piled up, Jenga-style, one on top of the next. All he could think about was Lily, inside the last vehicle, deliberately sent down there to die.

Bodie took hold of the wet guard rail, and started to work his way down. Twice, he almost slipped to his certain death, but he kept going. Suddenly, dangling from the crane at the Barton bridge came back to him, and he forced himself to wipe that from his mind. Slowly, very slowly, he got down to the almost vertical Mercedes, and opened the back left door. Ari and Sarah were there, terrified. Through the front seats, he could see Bill, distressed but hanging tough. Lily was hidden from Bodie's view, but she was there and it scared him to death that she was in danger.

'We have to climb away from here,' shouted Bodie, against the sound of the storm.

'Oh, my God!' cried Sarah. 'I can't do that.'

'Yes, you can, Sarah. Right now! Ari, pass your wife out to me.'

The Mercedes was creaking as it rested on the car below. Ari was as frightened as his wife, but he reassured her and made her leave the Mercedes, and ford the gap over to Bodie's grasp. Bodie pulled her tight and made her hold fast to the railings.

'Climb!' he ordered her. 'Climb, for Christ's sake!'

She started to pull herself up, with Bodie following, using his body to assist her efforts. At the top of the slope, Anthony appeared, and he reached down to lift Sarah as if she were a rag doll.

Bodie descended again. The wind tugged at his clothing. The seaspray threatened to loosen his grip. Back down at the Mercedes, he had expected Lily to appear next, but realised that she was holding back, probably too petrified.

'Ari! Your sister!?'

Ari was trying to pull Lily over him, but she was refusing. Harrison was out of the passenger side door.

'All you guys up!' shouted Bodie. 'I'll get Lily. Get out of here.'

Harrison, with only one good arm, appeared. He almost fumbled the leap across to the railings, but then Bodie had him by the belt and was pulling him up. Bill followed, and squeezed by Bodie.

Bodie reached for Ari, who would not leave his sister. 'Ari! She'll come for me. Get out now!'

Ari's hands reached out, clamping wrists with Bodie like Roman centurians offering greetings. Bodie got Ari onto the railings and shoved him upwards. Through the spray, he could see Anthony pulling Bill to safety.

'Lily! Lily, baby. Come to me.'

The Mercedes was quivering, its sheer weight starting to crush the car below. Bodie heard screaming from people down below. He leant as far as he could from the railings and looked into the back of the Mercedes. Lily was starting to come. They locked eyes, and she knew he would take care of her. She got her feet out over the wheel arch. She looked down.

'No!' shouted Bodie. 'Don't look down. Just look at me, baby.'

Bodie was stretching. Lily was easing out into the storm. Then she threw herself at him, and Bodie needed all his Freerunning skills and strength to keep his balance and swing her round until her feet found the metal.

'Climb now, baby,' he said to her ear, through her instantly soaked hair.

Bodie's body connected to Lily's, he forced her to put one hand over the next, one foot over the next, to ascend the ramp.

Surprising Bodie, Professor Siddiq was there, having descended part way down to reach Lily. It was brave of someone who had never climbed before. Both men used every last ounce of strength to get Lily over the top. As Bodie pulled himself to safety he saw Lily embracing Professor Siddiq for dear life. She did then reach back for him, but he waved them forward. 'Move!' he shouted.

# 27

Maria took care of Lily like a sister, putting her jacket round her shoulders and hugging her tight - for Lily, temperature-wise, it had been like being dumped through a hole in the ice at the Antarctic.

They found an unoccupied Portacabin office to shelter in. There were towels in the washroom, and they got out of their soaking top clothes. Professor Siddiq put on an oil-fired radiator, which took the chill off everyone. He continued to observe Lily.

Slowly the trauma of the event left them, and they were able to think straight once more, and to get some perspective back.

Harrison was stalking the room, thinking about the men who had deliberately directed them to their death. Crazy times brought on crazy actions. But they would have fled the scene. He just had to let the fury dissipate slowly.

Everyone else sat on the floor, relieved to have survived the Ramp of Death, but also realising that they were still in dire straits, stuck on the wrong side of the water. The weather was too bad, and there probably wasn't a ferry anywhere in port.

'Why are we trying to get to the Isle of Wight?' asked Aaron.

They had all forgotten that he was there. He had wrapped his jacket around Lily, and then settled down against the far wall.

'*What?*' asked Anthony, who was only slightly less aggravated than Harrison.

'Tell me exactly why, please.'

'To be inside a sealed environment. That way we don't get poisoned to death by your bloody government.'

'Well, as I see it, it's an international decision, but that's beside the point. If we need to be in an air-conditioned, sealed environment, why not just make for the Eden Project, in Cornwall?'

'The what?' asked Bodie.

'The Eden Project. I've been there. It's a garden, an experimental place with big air-conditioned domes. Like bubbles. They look like giant golf balls. Biomes, I think they call them. They have plants from all over the world.'

Sarah sat up. 'I'm very aware of that place, actually.'

'It rings a bell with me now,' said Anthony. He turned to Professor Siddiq. 'Professor?'

Professor Siddiq looked tired. He had Lily slumped against him. 'I don't know. It looks like we cannot get across to the Isle of Wight, after all. I don't know how much time we have left, but we might as well try for Cornwall.'

'Everyone agreed?' asked Anthony, turning in a circle.

Everyone nodded.

Anthony did a twelve-point turn, smashing into the car behind, to get the Porsche out of the queue to nowhere. Then Bill used his gun to hijack the first decent vehicle he spotted nearby, which was a VW Golf. It was cruel, but the family who owned the VW were left at the side of the road in the rain. Down the road two hundred metres, Bill stopped. Then he got out and ran back, with a bag of supplies, which he gave to the man of the family. He told him about the Portacabin, before running back to the VW.

Off they went to Cornwall, and it would be a drive through the night. Bill led the way, with Harrison navigating from an AA map on his lap. They took B roads along the coast, heading west, with a plan to join up with an A road at Bournemouth.

'What the hell is Cornwall, anyway?' asked Bill.

'Apparently, it's the last county in England.'

'I'm rapidly going off England.'

'I would go so far as to say I hate England. My granddaddy was here, during the Second World War. He flew a B-17 out of a base in Cambridgeshire. He always said he hated England. Warm beer and cold rain. He married an English girl, but... still.'

In the Porsche, Anthony had made hot air come through the air-con. Bodie was up beside him, while Professor Siddiq,

Maria and Aaron hunkered down in the back.

'How are you doing?' Anthony asked Bodie.

'I'm wrecked.'

'If they've blocked off the route to the Eden Project... Then, that's it?'

'Yeah, that's it. But at least we gave it a good go, cousin. And I'm glad I spent this time with you, man.'

'Me, too. Hey, I just had a thought. What if all this has just been a test? An exercise, to see if it could be done?'

'I don't think your contact in the US Navy thought it was a test when they murdered him.'

'No, of course not. I'm not thinking. I'm just tired.'

Aaron leant forward. 'If you're tired, let me drive?'

'No-one's driving my Porsche, but me. Anyway, are you even old enough to drive? Have you even got a licence?'

They all started laughing, and it carried on into hysterics.

Bill pulled the Golf into a petrol station. Anthony stopped behind it. Bill got out and gestured back at them that the needle was beyond low. While he started to fill the tank, Harrison went into the shop. Nobody else felt like entering another service station shop.

Harrison perused the newspapers, then took two cans of pop from the fridge and walked straight back out to Bill. They started to drink, while the petrol kept flowing. The woman cashier followed Harrison outside, to remonstrate with him over the theft. Harrison did his best to completely ignore the woman, and she eventually went back inside, probably to call the police. Bill finished filling the Golf's tank, and they were ready to move on, but then the cashier came storming back out, wielding a broom, which she began to whack Harrison with. He tried to fend her off, ducking and diving. He took several blows on his back, and one on his wounded shoulder, before finally reaching the sanctuary of the passenger seat. The cashier then went after Bill, trying to stop him shutting his door, but he managed to push the woman over onto her backside, slammed his car door, and off they went.

They continued to drive along the south coast of England, through Christchurch, Bournemouth and Dorchester. When they neared Exeter, in the early hours, Bill pulled over and the two Americans walked back for a conference.

'Okay,' said Harrison. 'So where's this Eden Project?'

Nobody in the Porsche actually knew, precisely. They all looked at Aaron.

'I got a bus there,' he defended himself.

There was still no internet access.

'We'll drive into Exeter,' suggested Anthony, 'and ask for help there.'

So they paused in Exeter city centre while Anthony sought directions. First, he encountered two blank teenage faces in a fast food outlet, and then an equally clueless cashier in a petrol station. It was a customer, paying for fuel, who provided the correct directions. Anthony thanked the man and jogged back out. That information put the Porsche back on point, and they pushed on towards Cornwall.

Bodie looked back at Maria. 'All right, kid?'

'I'm okay. Thank you.'

'Have you been to Cornwall before?'

'Yes, many times, on family holidays. Usually near St Ives

or Land's End.'

'Land's End?' asked Anthony. 'Sounds like the place to finally stop if we don't get into Eden.'

At Monza, just north of Milan, Italy, the Formula One Grand Prix took place that same day. It was a lovely, dry afternoon, with not a cloud in the sky, at one of the world's most famous races.

Into the fourteenth of fifty-three laps, Lewis Hamilton led Nico Rosberg, with Sebastian Vettel in third, which was quite normal. It was the fourth place runner who was making the fans stand up and cheer: Rio Haryanto, the exciting, new Indonesian driver, who was having a great race.

Haryanto lapped Max Verstappen, who was crawling back to the Pit with a  punctured left rear, and went around the Parabolica curve, still with Vettel in sight. He then went down the Home straight, where most of the fans were, in the bleachers. Vettel decided to pit, which left Haryanto in third, for the time being.

The Prime Minister of Italy stood up. He watched Vettel slow into the pits, then Haryanto flew by. He applauded gregariously. Then he turned to his female assistant, who gave a slight nod; it was definitely time to leave. The helicopter was ready. Without saying a word to other, startled, guests in the VIP area of the main stand, the Prime Minister, and all his entourage, simply left.

Haryanto carried on. He passed a couple of back-markers. Rosberg was twenty seconds ahead of him. Not to worry about that. Keep doing the correct things. Keep concentrating. He was loving it. Through the first Lesmo corner he went, then into the second Lesmo at 200kph. Immediately, in front of him, in the middle of the track, stood a woman, head to toe in a black burka. Haryanto, like all racing drivers, possessed superhuman reactions, but he had to decide even quicker that he would not hit and kill the woman instantly, instead, turning the wheel hard left, making the car leave the track, skim across the gravel, before destroying itself on the far barrier in a spectacular crash, with race marshals diving for cover.

Yellow lights flashed onto the warning screens, initially. The race was neutralised for safety reasons. It would soon be stopped. Italian police were rushing to detain the woman on the track. Haryanto's car was a complete write-off, but the safety shell had saved his life. He unbuckled himself, stepped from the steaming heap of carbon fibre  and rubber, and allowed marshals to take him through a gap in the wall. As he went, he was trying to look back for the woman in the burka.

# 28

Anthony drove them down the road which ran beside the Dartmoor National Park, where the scenery was exceptionally beautiful, in the dawn sunshine. Not long after, they went straight through the city of Plymouth. Soon, they hit Cornwall, and were out onto smaller, more rural roads, which were typical of the most picturesque county in the whole of England.

Anthony and Bodie were constantly conferring over the route, and looking at road signs. They were satisfied that they were heading, generally, in the right direction. At one stage they found themselves frustratingly behind a slow-moving caravan, with no way to pass.

'Caravanners want shooting,' said Bodie, half joking.

Maria gasped, pretending to be shocked. 'Bodie.'

'But they do. They've always needed to be taken out of the gene pool. They are complete traffic hold-uppers.'

They saw signs for Bodmin.

'*Doc Martin*,' said Anthony.

Maria laughed, but Aaron was puzzled.

'It's a popular British TV show,' she explained. 'Based near here.'

A sign showed St Austell. 'That's what we need,' said Anthony. 'Once we get near to there, we need to ask directions again. No doubt this place is going to be in the middle of bloody nowhere.'

In the end, they didn't need to ask, as just outside the small town of St Blazey, they saw a sign for the Eden Project. Spirits lifted in the Porsche. Still they got a little lost, twisting and turning down tiny country lanes. Another sign set them buzzing again. Anthony drove on faster.

'Come on!' shouted Anthony, geeing himself up.

He slowed, turned left, being careful to avoid a stationary tractor. It was then that they got their first shock: lying on the ground were two farmers. Joy turned instantly to fear, as they drove past the corpses.

It was happening. It was actually happening.

Anthony gunned the Porsche down the road.

'Where is it?' asked Professor Siddiq. 'Where is the place?'

Hedgerow after hedgerow flashed by. Desperation was setting in. They saw another dead person: an elderly hiker, collapsed backwards onto his rucksack, his boots in the air. Terror came to Anthony's driving, thinking that at any second he could succumb to whatever it was that had been released into the atmosphere, and he would crash into a tree, and that would be that.

They broke out, briefly, into wider countryside, just in time to see a male corpse about to crash its microlight aircraft. What a bizarre sight - Anthony slowed, staring - what an absolutely bizarre sight, and then the hedgerows closed in again.

Anthony took another left, and had to slam on the brakes, shocked to be faced by a living, moving human being, even if it was only a Police Community Support Officer, in his blue-banded cap, white shirt and badly fitting pants, with a raised hand, demanding that he stop. Beyond the man, there had been a bad road accident, something had crashed into a milk tanker.

Very reluctantly, Anthony brought down his window.

'I'm sorry,' said the PCSO. 'There are fatalities, following a road traffic accident. You'll have to turn back. I'm waiting for the local police to arrive.'

'Can we not just squeeze past?'

The PCSO sniffed. 'Well, apart from being grossly insensitive, sir, it's a crime scene. So, you'll have to turn around.'

Professor Siddiq stood from the Porsche. He approached the young PCSO, then punched the man three times in the head, knocking him out onto the grass verge. Professor Siddiq retook his seat, without a word, and Anthony began to squeeze the Porsche around the fairly grim accident scene. Maria turned her head away, not wanting to see, while everybody else looked closely: the tanker driver was dead in the mangled remains of his cabin. There were six corpses in the wreckage of a smashed up, pale blue VW camper van; four young males in the back, and an older, obese couple, covered head to toe in blood, looking like they had gone through the windscreen.

They were glad to leave the gruesome scene behind them, and Anthony sped onwards.

'Stop!' cried Aaron. 'For the love of God, stop.'

At a United Nations refugee camp, just north of Izmir, in Turkey, the day had started out cold and dry. People wandered about between the regimented white huts and the white tents. Children finished a class, and came out to play.

Bashir Zuabi, and his wife, Yana, watched the children scampering about. A football appeared and became the focus of the fun. It made them smile, at a time when they had very little to smile about. They had lost their small son, Adnan, just before fleeing their home town of Al Bab, in Syria. Bashir and Yana, both thirty-eight, had already made the crossing to the Greek island of Lesbos, only to be sent back. That had been six months ago. Since then, they had just existed. They looked at each other; soul-mates. The ball, followed by a number of children, found its way into their legs, making them laugh. Then the children fell down. The ball rolled away. Bashir and Yana stopped focussing on their love for each other, and realised that the children at their feet were no longer moving. Nor were any of the children nearby. Mercifully, the horrible sight was extremely brief for the couple, before they themselves slumped to the ground.

Brothers, Alberto and Tobias Chiponde, and five accomplices, had crossed the border from Mozambique into Tanzania overnight. They were taking their usual route, hunting for ivory. They knew the risks, especially with the new government directive that all poachers were to be shot on sight; but they were heavily armed themselves, with Kalashnikovs and shotguns. These days, the wardens were using drones and light aircraft to try to spot them, but so far they had remained undisturbed. They would fight to the death, if they had to - the rewards were so great.

They had started tracking the herd of elephant just after sun-up. As soon as they could, they started to close in, gradually; a bull elephant and two females being their initial target. The first priority was to avoid making a mistake and getting trampled to death. Then, once in position, to strike quickly and simultaneously. Alberto looked over to Tobias, squatting in the bush. Then he checked to his other side, seeing an aimed rifle poking out from behind a tree. The bull knew they were there, he was starting to get agitated. He would protect his family, if he could. Alberto was ready. He looked again for the rifle, but could not see it. Never mind, his colleague would be ready for his signal. He looked again at Tobias, but his brother was lying on the floor. *Tobias?* Both horrified and puzzled, Alberto began to move towards Tobias, but made only three steps before collapsing, dead before he hit the floor. The magnificent bull elephant took one last look at them, then moved gracefully on with his family.

Lincolnshire farmer, Guy Thomas Walker, was repairing the damage to his bridge over the Hobhole drain at Old Leake. He had parked his Land Rover and examined all the skid marks nearby, then puzzled over what seemed to be shell casings lying on the floor- he had no interest in guns, didn't even own a shotgun, or go shooting socially, but had seen enough films in his time to be able to recognise them. He wondered whether it was worth bothering the police about. He took off his flat cap and scratched his head.

He then waved at a passing neighbour, on a tractor, before continuing to rebuild some more of the dry stone walling of the bridge. He wondered what to have for lunch. Then he sat down. It was while thinking about why he was suddenly sitting down, that he stopped thinking altogether, and slowly slumped forward onto his face.

Inside the Eco-town, on the Isle of Wight, Dr and Vivienne Rhodes, Margaret and Barry Fallon, and the Jordan family were all seated together, eating a meal. They were in a massive canteen, with perhaps three hundred other people. It was noisy, especially with the sound of clashing cutlery.

They were just beginning to come to terms with what was happening to them. They had not been told anything official about the crisis, and had chosen to ignore the wilder rumours flying around the dormitories. There were police patrols walking about, and a number of people had been warned over their disruptive behaviour.

Sitting not too far away, was the Prime Minister, eating with his wife and several Cabinet members. Nobody was talking, and the Prime Minister appeared sombre. A young Aide approached and whispered something into the Prime Minister's ear. The Prime Minister nodded his thanks, checked his watch, then continued with his meal.

After Aaron had shouted for them to stop the Porsche, Anthony skidded into a dramatic halt, leaving tyre marks on the road. Bill braked, and pulled in behind them.

'Let me find this place,' begged Aaron. 'Please, let me find it.'

Aaron went to the boot and brought out his drone. He placed it gently on the road and fired it up. Nobody else got out of the vehicles. They watched the drone rise above the hedgerows. Aaron returned to his place in the rear of the Porsche, looking at the pictures on the screen, sent back from the camera - green field after green field. He took it higher and turned it 360 degrees. Into shot, perhaps a mile and a half away, came the distinctive golf ball shapes, and the cultured landscape of the Eden Project.

'Go! Go!' said Aaron. 'Try to bear right when you can.'

Anthony drove, with Aaron directing him. They passed more corpses on the ground, with living people standing over them, puzzled and horrified, until they themselves succumbed and collapsed down.

Faster and faster, Anthony drove, even though he thought of those poor people in the VW Camper van - they had known, and were only trying to save themselves. Aaron continued to call out directions, and then the two cars reached the entrance to the Eden Project, screeching to a stop. Here, again, was the scene of living people finding dead people lying on the ground, and trying to reach the emergency services on their cells, without any signal.

'Move!' Anthony shouted at his passengers, flinging open his own door.

Aaron jumped out, carelessly dropping his handset, and nearby the drone came straight down with a crash.

Lily, and the others from the Golf, all carrying supplies, rushed to join up with the first group.

'In! In!' shouted Anthony.

Anthony looked back briefly, seeing all the people now on the floor, and then he ran after the others. There was a black, female member of staff, initially observing the incident of the people on the ground, who then watched the mad group arriving like bats out of hell. She was manhandled by Anthony and carried into the reception building, complaining bitterly and loudly.

'Shut up and listen,' Anthony told her, putting her down. 'Shut up.'

Livid at being assaulted, she would not be quiet, until Maria stepped in to slap her hard across the face.

Anthony brought out his gun and pointed it at her. 'Take us into a sealed dome. Do it right now and we all might live.'

The terrified woman, whose name badge called her Tanisha, led them quickly through the complex, down a corridor with wandering tourists all about, and through into one of the famous golf ball biomes. It looked like a rainforest. They stepped out onto a large decked area, feeling the different, hotter temperature, and looked out over the shrubbery and trees. A number of tourists were walking about, down on the floor below.

Anthony turned Tanisha to him. 'Are we sealed inside here?'

'Yes,' she answered, in a sulk. 'Well, almost. Maintenance have gone up to clean the outside roof.'

Tanisha pointed, and all their eyes followed, to an empty workmen's cradle, on a rail which ran the length of the structure, and above which there showed a patch of blue sky through an opening in the bubble.

'Bodie,' said Anthony, distraught at the sight of the gap in the ceiling.

Bodie had already reacted, climbing the metal frame of the building. The higher he went, the more it curved inwards, increasing the dangerous pull of gravity on his body. Everyone watched him go, from strut to strut. Maria and Lily embraced without even knowing it, watching their man risk his life for them. Bodie moved quickly, taking risks, using all his muscles, sensing the mounting danger. Still he went up, to around 50m high, starting to sweat in the rainforest humidity, his hands slippy on the steel. He swung his body over and managed to land on the cradle. From a kneeling position, he looked up at the opening, never being so frightened before in his life. There was a small metal ladder. He went up and popped his head through. There was no wind, but the blue sky filled his world. It was beautiful up there. Suddenly he felt a rush - a simple joy at being alive.

He caught a quick glimpse of two maintenance men lying motionless on the roof of the biome, and, passing overhead on a tourist attraction zipwire, a clearly dead teenage boy flew by, which was quite an obscene sight. Bodie, expecting to die with every new breath he took, yanked the hexagonal flap upwards, and brought it down into place on top of his head. As it seemed to seal itself in place, Bodie was so relieved. He slid down the ladder and sat on the base of the cradle, enjoying the simple pleasure of being out of breath.

# 29

Dr and Vivienne Rhodes, Margaret and Barry Fallon, and the Jordan family all stayed together, in the massive administration and canteen complex, while they awaited their turn to be given temporary housing, down in the valley - apparently, and unsurprisingly, there was a huge backlog. 'Usual British government incompetence...' Barry had grumbled.

The rumour came near to them again, from various people, and they were just starting to digest the awful possibility of it being true - the Jordan girls would have looked for it on the internet, but they were frustrated and not enjoying the technology blackout.

The Prime Minister was no longer showing himself in

public; which was noticeable - apparently, there had been some kind of confrontation with a group of people wanting answers, and his security detail had needed to step in. There were, however, a number of celebrities coming and going; people they had only ever seen on television or at the cinema. Autographs were being requested and selfies being taken with them. If the celebrities knew the full story of what was going on, then they were not showing it.

Margaret stood up and asked if anyone wanted more tea. Only Barry held out his cup. She went over to the food counter. From there she could look through the large plate glass windows, down over the entire valley. The light was unusual, but apart from that, it looked beautiful. The woman behind the counter, who was called Jean,  served someone their meal, then watched Margaret using one of the tea urns.

'Are you still waiting, love?' asked Jean.

'We might be sleeping in here,' replied Margaret.

'Well, you'll be first for breakfast,' laughed Jean.

Margaret laughed. 'Yes. That's true'

It was from over Jean's head that Margaret first spotted the flames; orange and black, rolling along the ceiling of the huge kitchen. Chefs and waiters started running in all directions, and then the fire alarm sounded. Jean turned to look, and was knocked backwards into her industrial-sized tray of Cottage pie by the force of the heat. Margaret fell down to the carpet in shock. There was screaming everywhere, the water sprinklers came on, but the flame and smoke already engulfed the top half of the single-level complex. Panic ensued, people running, hoping to find an exit. Barry Fallon came to Margaret, dragged her to her feet, and then in a deep stoop, as the toxic smoke was appalling, they headed to where an open fire door had created a funnel of fleeing bodies.

They got "outside", seeing the army rushing to tackle the fire, as best they could. Dr Rhodes and his wife were there, helping with the victims of smoke inhalation, but none of the Jordan family were anywhere to be seen. Barry and Margaret sat down on a free bit of ground and looked back, at what was now a raging inferno.

'Are you all right, darling?' asked Barry.

Margaret coughed a little, but she felt all right. She would have responded to her husband, if they had not realised that the Prime Minister, all his Cabinet members, uniformed top military brass, and several famous celebrities, happened to have gathered alongside where they sat. They were all staring in disbelief at the fire. That was not part of the master plan.

'We had a lucky escape there, darling,' said Barry.

'You think, Barry?'

Margaret watched the smoke and flame, with nowhere to go but straight up, like a volcano. Clearly, there had been no proper planning for fire protection. The Prime Minister had a horrified, resigned look on his face, while a grim General whispered something into his ear.

The fire, smoke and great heat reached the ceiling of the eco-dome, and the day started to turn to night. Slowly the roof began to blister and bubble, then catch fire, and started to fail in one hexagonal unit after the next. People fled. But there was nowhere to flee to. They were all back in the real, poisoned world, with everybody else.

Lily sat on the floor of the Rainforest biome together with Aaron. The American had turned his cap back to front, and was playing footsie with her boots. What a rush that had been. *Were they safe now? Would they survive?* They were supposed to be checking supplies, but just wanted to sit for a while. Gather themselves. Lily smiled at him, then glanced at a passing Professor Siddiq, who was walking with Tanisha, trying to make the woman understand what was happening.

Lily turned her head the other way: Anthony was playing I-spy with some of the tourist children, while their shocked parents were standing around in deep discussion. Harrison and Bill could be seen in a café area, making hot drinks for everyone. Behind her, Lily knew that her brother and sister-in-law were cuddled up together on a bench.

And there was Bodie, her Bodie, sitting with Maria, her legs over his, talking softly, occasionally kissing. They made such a lovely couple. Lily smiled, so happy for him.

Later on, Bodie found Lily, sitting quietly on a bench, staring into the green foliage, and they embraced in a lovely way. Then they looked into each other's eyes.

'Are you okay?' he asked, cupping her small jaw.

'Yes. Yes, I think so.'

'Good.'

There were two families in there with them, the Brandons from Kidderminster, and the Lewis-Alukos from Swindon, totalling four adults and six children. It had not been difficult to convince the tourists of the truth, especially as they could see the outlines of the dead men on the roof. Everyone sat about having the strangest little picnic of their lives.

Afterwards, Bodie joined Anthony up on the highest viewing platform, amid the canopy of leaves. Through the blurred wall, they believed they could just make out a great many bodies lying on the ground, just outside. Both men were relaxed and calm, after such an amazing adventure.

'So, cousin,' said Bodie. 'We made it this far.'

'So we did,' answered Anthony.

They both leant on the wooden railing. It was a nice change to be able to stay still for a while. Anthony closed his eyes for a moment. Bodie looked down at their fellow survivors; Maria was teaching the children to play *Go Boom*. The three Americans were talking together, over coffee. Lily, his Lily, was chatting intimately with Professor Siddiq.

Anthony stretched, then looked at Bodie, slapping his younger cousin on the shoulder.

'So?' asked Bodie. They were both ready to have a good laugh. 'How long do you want to wait?'

Gunfight at the Old Leake Canal

GB Hope

Made in the USA
Charleston, SC
15 May 2016